# *Leadership*
## Is Concept Heavy

A Case Against Fragmented
Theories in Evolutionary and
Contemporary Leadership

## DR. ENOCH ANTWI

authorHOUSE®

*AuthorHouse™*
*1663 Liberty Drive*
*Bloomington, IN 47403*
*www.authorhouse.com*
*Phone: 1 (800) 839-8640*

*Published by AuthorHouse  04/20/2017*

*ISBN: 978-1-5246-8885-1 (sc)*
*ISBN: 978-1-5246-8886-8 (hc)*
*ISBN: 978-1-5246-8884-4 (e)*

*Library of Congress Control Number: 2017906045*

*Print information available on the last page.*

*Any people depicted in stock imagery provided by Thinkstock are models, and such images are being used for illustrative purposes only. Certain stock imagery © Thinkstock.*

*This book is printed on acid-free paper.*

This book is dedicated to my mother,
who would sell all her property and do any menial job to send me
to school;

the many communities and institutions and organizations I have
had the opportunity to lead;

and to my resourceful wife, Bertha,
and our three kids, Eldridge, Shealtiel, and Elbridge,
who will not let me sleep at night.

# INTRODUCTION

## SMALL ISSUES

A newly wedded couple entered into a lovely agreement. The groom told his bride, "I will take care of every 'big issue' in the house, while you take care of all 'small issues.'"

The innocent wife agreed.

They had already made partial payment for the wedding reception. When the outstanding bill for the wedding reception was due, the man said, "Oh! This is a small issue; you have to pay."

The wife obliged.

Subsequently, all utility bills, insurance, groceries, and any other expenditure became the responsibility of the wife because the husband said they were all small issues. Unable to contain it anymore, she discussed it with her mother.

The mother visited the couple one evening and asked her son-in-law, "Tell me what the big issues are."

Her son-in-law responded, "Wars in Syria, Iraq, Afghanistan, Somalia, and Sudan; earthquakes in Haiti and Costa Rica; tsunamis, tornadoes, demonstrations in Egypt's Tahrar Square; Russia taking over the Crimea; the recent presidential election in the United States—"

"Wait a minute!" The mother-in-law interrupted him in the middle of the narration to ask a simple question. "If you come home from work and there is no food on the table, will that be a big issue or small issue?"

The man replied, "That will be the biggest issue ... in this house."

## The How and Why: Small or Big?

Good leaders understand the use of how and why in solving day-to-day challenges at work. However, a respectable number of leaders ignore the how and why of "small issues" to concentrate on the "big issues." Many leaders have a standard unto themselves and judge employees by a separate standard. For some leaders, popular and accomplished colleagues remain inspirations and role models. Others define their own shared values and handle fear based on personal instincts, experience, and the amount of thinking they put into the situation. Yet other leaders pat themselves at the back when they manage to get things right and celebrate achievements when bigger dreams and aspirations are achieved. Often, the small issues are unintentionally pushed under the rug.

On countless occasions, leaders struggle to satisfy their own dreams, disregarding the dreams of their followers. An example will suffice in explaining this concept. In 1923, a group of great leaders and rich businessmen met at the Edgewater Beach Hotel in Chicago. Among them were Charles Schwab, head of the largest independent company; Samuel Insull, president of the world's largest utility at that time; Howard Hopson, the head of the largest gas company at that time; and Richard Whitney, president of the New York Stock Exchange, among others. Twenty-five years later, four of these leaders ended their lives as follows: Schwab died penniless after living for five years on borrowed money; Insull died broke in a foreign land; Hopson went insane; and Whitney was released from jail (Kiyosaki 2012).

Today, we live in times of greater and faster change than these men did, and that means the struggle to satisfy personal and leadership dreams can be more daunting. Assessing leadership within the context of functions that individual leaders perform is part of the formula, for leadership struggles tend to be the result of limited knowledge and ignorance. As an example, a leadership behavior that remains a mere extension of the old patron approach, rather than partnering with followers and employees, is bound to fail. Such leadership becomes as easily predictable as the ending of a movie in which a mother rejects her pregnant teen daughter, and the scorned daughter eventually becomes a medical doctor who cures her mother of cancer.

People are used to things that are similar to individual ideas of natural life situations. Leadership itself is a familiar endeavor in daily activities in homes, faith-based institutions, associations, institutions, organizations, interactions, discussions, and politics. It is often easy to recognize "good leadership" in modern situations. Thus, it is important for leaders not to play a role different from their character, for that is a mismatch. In any case, when leaders play roles when they are in character, how do we expect them to play that role as though they are *not* in character?

A comedy actor and an instructor at my former college provided an explanation to this quandary: "Whenever people tell me I am funny, I am happy because it means I am playing my role quite well."

Leaders must be authentic and bring what they do to life. There must be natural response to what leaders do—just like we expect to see in everyday life. Many individuals can tell a good leader from a bad one based on many constructs. Some individuals judge leaders based on perceptions or opinions; others on facts. Still others judge leaders on issues beyond the leader's control and capabilities and still expect the leader to take responsibility for his or her actions. The solution lies in how leaders take care of "small issues," both at home and work, because both situations (home and work) affect effective leadership.

# CONTENTS

# CHAPTER 1

## EVOLUTIONARY (NATURAL) SCIENCE VERSUS SOCIAL SCIENCE

The concept of *ignorant leadership* is the honest understanding that leaders cannot know everything in the organization. According to Stacey (2001), leaders cannot know everything even if they devote to lifelong learning in a given organization. Furthermore, different combinations of situational elements, forces, and conditions continue to create continuums in leadership, learning, and behaviors that make it difficult for leaders to grasp the complex theories and learning in organizations (Senge 1990). Leadership is concept heavy. A leader who cannot generate multiple ideas and multiple solutions is limited in knowledge. Admitting a limitation of knowledge and ideas is not ignorance; it is astute knowledge. It helps the leader to remove three mental blocks—failure to see, failure to move, and failure to cross the finish line—of gaining new knowledge and implementing new ideas (Black and Gregerson 2014).

Chapter 1 develops a framework for conceptualizing research on a new concept of ignorant leadership and examines the reasons many organizational leaders are ignorant of what they do. The author has presented these thoughts at the peer-reviewed conferences of the Association of Politics and Life Sciences (APLS), of which he is a member in good standing. Research presentations at this conference are evolutionarily inclined. However, the author, through literature and research, observed that leadership concepts in evolutionary sciences are similar to present-day social science concepts of

1

leadership. This study expands both concepts and makes a case against fragmented leadership models and theories.

## The Case against Fragmented Leadership Models and Theories

Leadership study permeates biology and politics (sometimes referred to as "biopolitics") and speaks to many linkages between the life sciences and the study of political, business, community, nonprofit, or religious leadership. Policy implications emerging from the life sciences and political and biological influences, as well as from community and religious institutions, create complexity and fragmentation in leadership studies. Admitting to situational inclinations of leadership studies, it is academically thoughtful to point out that there are irreconcilable leadership theories that are difficult to characterize and comprehend (Hogg 2001; Northouse 2010). Multiple definitions of leadership, each written from a different viewpoint and with different emphasis (Chan 2005), and different expectations from different leaders in global leadership studies (Bird 2008; Zaccaro 2007), create a perceived fragmentation. Moreover, most leadership theories are too vague and shallow to support empirical research (Northouse 2010). In some cases, there is inadequate understanding of what differentiates good leaders from bad leaders (Harshman and Harshman 2008).

In a transformational leadership study, Bass and Avolio (1994) argued that transformational leaders build leader-follower relationships based on mutual encouragement characterized by the leader's personality, inspiration, and intellectual motivation to transform not only situations but also followers. A different charismatic leadership study (Rowold and Heinitz 2007) found that leaders and followers develop unique relationships based directly on the leader's personality, often in the face of a lack of proven skills or any meaningful experience.

The missing piece in the studies cited above is how to prove a skill or meaningful experience of a leader's influence on followers to an evolutionary scientist (van Vugt 2011). Other researchers, such as Hogg (2001), argued that there is difficulty in developing a leadership selection process or even predicting a successful and effective leader with substantial accuracy based on any of the numerous and separate leadership theories. The problem appears even more complicated by the complex nature of direct and indirect leadership roles and behavioral or relational expectations of the different leadership concepts.

In what appears to be a response to Hogg's assertion, Solansky (2008) opined that even if an efficient process could be used to select effective leaders, the dynamics of leadership situations might render the selection invalid. On the other hand, Bird (2011) argued that there is not a single, best way to lead but that leadership remains situational in both local and global contexts. Bird's (2011) positionality notwithstanding, it is important for leadership researchers and practitioners to develop an integrated and coherent common understanding of leadership for effective organizational learning and practices (Burns 1978). Of course, the differences are quite understandable, considering the complexity of human behavior and many unmeasured variables in leadership models. However, the differences also confuse not only scholars and practitioners but also the ordinary person on the street, who passionately wants to understand leadership. From this argumentative standpoint, the status quo is wrong.

## Why the Status Quo Is Wrong

Contrasting lists of essential traits that cast doubt on the empirical status of trait theories (Bass and Bass 2008), behavioral studies focus on the "external" behavior of leaders rather than "internal" traits, beliefs, and motives (Northouse 2010). Most leadership findings are survey data and not replicable experiments (Hazy, Goldstein, and Lichtenstein 2007). Furthermore, inadequate understanding of the following—the whats and whys of leaders' behavior, inadequate knowledge of what essential behaviors comprise leadership, and inadequate frameworks of how researchers and practitioners differentiate between formal and informal relationships of leaders and followers (Burns 1978)—thereby make the status quo wrong.

According to Latour (2000), there appears to be a misunderstanding about what it means to provide a social explanation of a piece of science. Latour (2000) further argued that the social sciences imitate the natural sciences in a way that renders them unable to profit from the type of objectivity found in the natural sciences. Thus, the meaning of "social" and of "science" should be reconfigured before the definition of what a social science is and what it can do in the leadership arena is considered (Latour 2000). This author disagrees with Latour (2000) that only the natural scientist is "in the know" of producing solid, objective, and verifiable knowledge of social phenomena. It appears that both natural scientists and social scientists are either ignorant of each other's philosophical commitments or do not want to accept each other's worldview.

Even though this study admits that neither of the approaches is superior to the other, reconciling the two approaches could reunite leadership theories and break them into simple concepts for easy understanding.

## Weber on Natural Science and Social Science

Weber (1946) rejected the contention that the cognitive aims of the natural and the social sciences were basically the same. According to Weber, it is impossible to make legitimate generalizations, because human actions are not subject to the regularities that govern the world of nature. Weber (1947) further argued that the method of science—whether subject matter, things, or people—always precedes abstraction and generalization. Thus, Weber (1947) took the stand

4

that people, in contrast to things, could be understood not only in external manifestations of behavior but also in the underlying motivations. According to Weber (1947), differences between the natural sciences and the social sciences arise from differences in the cognitive intentions of the researcher. Thus, the natural scientist is primarily interested in those aspects of natural events that can be formulated in terms of abstract laws, while the social scientist may wish to search for such lawful abstract generalizations in human behavior (Weber 1947). Therefore, making value judgments of which approach is "better" seems a futile effort. However, an integrated approach to reconcile the two methods could make leadership studies stimulating while creating a common understanding among leadership practitioners.

## Fundamental Premise

If we continue to use current fragmented leadership models and theories, we are not likely to solve the challenge of leadership soon.

## Think Links

According to Carter, Bishop, and Kravits (2012), a *think link* (also known as a *mind map*) is a visual form of note-taking that encourages flexible thinking. The visual design makes the connections easy to see as well as shape the visualized pictures beyond words. Carter et al. (2012) explained that to create a think link, one should start by circling or boxing a topic in the middle of a sheet of paper. Next, a line is drawn from the topic to write the name of one major idea at the end of the line. The major idea is circled. Specific facts related to the main idea are linked with dotted lines. The process is continued, connecting thoughts to one another with circles, lines, and words to make meaning. Think link also supports reflection and recollection of information.

This study proposes leadership studies to be think links connecting the different natural and social scientific thoughts with circles, lines, and words for an integrated study. Though challenging, think links could present a clearer understanding of leadership studies and practices to the layperson. The unconnected leadership ideas continue to present a distorted visualized picture of what leadership is about. A tree with trunk, branches, and roots as a central concept appears clearer than another tree presented in a fragmented concept. Admittedly, leadership concepts could be difficult to construct as a think link. However, as emphasized earlier, scholars' and practitioners' honest attempts toward linking natural-science concepts with social-science theories on leadership could create better understanding in learning of the subject.

## Research Shortfall: Reasons for Leadership Gaps

According to Johnson (2007), a leader's self-confidence could lead to self-ignorance. Self-ignorance might lead to trustworthiness issues with followers. A leader who is not trustworthy could become assertive and intolerant and still lose the respect of followers. The tolerant leader may be indecisive and unconvincing because of a lack of knowledge in the subject under discussion. The decisive one might not communicate clearly because of a lack of communication skills. Leaders who communicate clearly might also not listen if they lack active listening skills (Spears 2002). Leaders who listen might not inspire followers, because they might not be able offer wise solutions (Sternberg 2008). The inspiring leaders might not be good relationship builders because they lack emotional intelligence (Goleman 1997).

Furthermore, good relationship builders could be unethical, because they have little knowledge about ethical values and theories (Price 2006). Ethical leaders could be inauthentic, because they lack spiritual propriety or their spiritual life is private and separate from their espoused public behavior (Boa 2001; Lambert 2009). Authentic leaders might not respect diversity, because they have no idea what "diversity" means in a complex, globalized world of leadership (Bird and Osland 2004).

Therefore, again, if leadership researchers, scholars, and practitioners continue to use fragmented leadership theories and models in leadership studies, it is not likely to solve the challenge of leadership soon, because of the visibly interpretation gaps between life science and social science (Harshman and Harshman 2008; Vogt and Ahuja 2011).

## Closing the Gap: Life Science and Social Science

In an organizational-system theory, Daft (2009) contended that environmental context and design are part of leadership. Goldstein and Lichtenstein (2007) also found that abilities play important roles in leadership. Harshman and Harshman (2008) also argued that not every leadership experience is developmental. However, van Vugt and Ahuja (2011) conceptualized that many leadership experiences lead to personal and developmental skills. Interest seems to be a driving force that pulls leaders and followers in when completing a given assignment or executing a task effectively in an experiential situation (van Vugt and Ahuja 2011). Thus, interest could be a prime force of creativity or energy in developing personal leadership skills and style to close the natural and social leadership gap.

Moreover, a leader's personality style could depend on how he or she interacts naturally and easily with others (Goldstein and Lichtenstein 2007). Therefore, families and environments in which an individual interacts naturally could also play an influencing role in the individual's understanding of work values and worldviews of both the natural and social sciences (Goldstein and Lichtenstein 2007; Harshman and Harshman 2008). The knowledge and understanding could bridge the *ignorance gap* of each of the sciences. The gap appears wider when evolutionary thoughts and sociological concepts of leadership, in their unique ways, try to make sense in a quest of understanding leadership skills, traits, relationships, and values in modern societies. Little is known, for instance, of a life science theory of evolutionary leadership in contemporary organizational leadership (van Vugt 2011). Therefore, a critical look at an evolutionary path of leadership could throw more light on the need for an integrated approach in understanding leadership through the filters of natural-science and social-science leadership experiences. This path must be threaded with no personal bias or parochial interest, but rather with an open mind to deal with the fundamental topic of this study, the conscious or unconscious *ignorance* of the other side of the scientific viewpoint.

## Evolutionary Path of Leadership

Evolutionary theory conceptualizes how the role of food sharing may have seeded the beginning of leadership and policymaking by teaching apes and humans how to forge alliances and coalitions (van Vugt 2011). This means leadership and followership arose in human species in response to survival and reproductive challenges (Van Vugt and Ahuja 2011). According to Kellerman (2004), the Great Man Theory and subsequent leadership theory replacements (such as transformational leadership, transactional leadership, authentic leadership, ethical leadership, situational leadership, steward leadership, servant leadership, charismatic leadership, and so forth) only highlighted good leadership and ignored bad leadership.

Van Vugt and Ahuja (2011) seemed to support Kellerman's 2004 assertion by conceptualizing that bad leadership is explained via a mismatch hypothesis or chasm between humans' slowly evolving brains and rapidly evolving culture. Thus, evolutionary researchers argue that the prescriptive formula to fight bad leadership is to align human leadership with biological anchorage, because only human leadership and biological anchorages could explain the what and why of leaders (van Vugt and Ahuja 2011). However, this assertion faces numerous challenges.

## Challenges of the Evolutionary Path of Leadership

There are many unexplained fundamental details in the evolutionary path of understanding leadership as posited by van Vugt and Ahuja (2011):

(a) Ancient nomadic survival through hunting is not identical to modern flourishing cities of economic and social activities.
(b) The power of modern technology, information, communication, and transportation makes modern leadership more complex than ancient leadership.
(c) There is conflicting knowledge of social behaviors of apes and early hominids.
(d) Some evolutionary theory languages could be described by social-scientist theorists as "over the top."
(e) Many business scholars and professionals are unfamiliar with knowledge of life science's thought processes of evolutionary leadership, which might lead to hostility of biological explanations of the social leadership phenomenon.
(f) Empirical evidence to confirm or disconfirm either a good-natured or bad-natured hypothesis remains elusive in evolutionary studies.
(g) Debate on the degree of evolutionary continuity or discontinuity between apes and Pleistocene hunter-gatherer forbears is not clear.
(h) Genetics and life experiences alone do not program leaders to lead (Goldstein and Lichtenstein 2007; van Vugt and Ahuja 2011).

## Making Sense of Natural- and Social-Science Experiences

It appears that the future of making sense in leadership studies rests in integrating natural- and social-scientific theories into an all-inclusive leadership study (Burns 1978; Bailey and Axerold 2001). A reconciled approach could appeal to both sides of the sciences.

Fortunately, leadership is not an issue of "the only tool one has is a hammer," in which every situation is treated as a nail (Harshman and Harshman 2008). If leadership theorists have more tools in natural and social sciences, why not accept, appreciate, adjust, and adapt to each appropriate concept in an integrated approach embedded in complex adaptive systems of leadership (Sargut and McGrath 2011)?

## Building Blocks: Ten Recommendations of Evolutionary Leadership Theory

According to van Vugt and Ahuja (2011), there are ten recommendations of evolutionary leadership theory:

1) Do not overrate the romance of leadership.
2) Find a niche and develop your prestige.
3) Keep it small and natural.
4) Favor followers.
5) Practice distributed leadership.
6) Mind the pay gap.
7) Look for leaders within.
8) Watch out for nepotism.
9) Avoid the dark side.
10) Do not judge a leader by their appearance.

## Is There Any Link?

It appears most of the ten recommendations of evolutionary leadership above resonate well among contemporary leadership scholars. For instance, overrating the romance of leadership could lead to bad leadership (Kellerman 2004). Kotter and Cohen's (2004) second step of the eight steps of change also appears to support the act of finding a niche to develop a leader's prestige. According to Kotter and Cohen's second step of change, the process entails creating a guiding coalition by putting together a group with enough power to lead change and getting the group to work together as a team. Therefore, if social-science theories of leadership resonate well with evolutionary tenets, it seems logical to argue from the premise that fragmented views could do more harm than good in leadership studies and practices (Burns 1978; van Vugt and Ahuja 2011). If the premise holds true, could there be empirical challenges of various leadership theories taught in business schools without scientific components? If that is the case, can the situation be reviewed and adapted? Does the situation become more complex and controversial? Could the right answers be poked in the middle of the complexity? Who should poke first? And who will respond? Should it be the natural-science community or the social-science community?

## Poking the Middle of Complexity: Complex System Adaptive Theory

Complexity theories originated from physics, computer science, mathematical, and biological research (Cardwell 2005). According to Sargut and McGrath (2011), a system consists of many moving parts and possible interactions that operate in patterned ways. Relationships in complex adaptive systems (including organizations) are nonlinear and are made up of numerous interconnections and divergent choices that create unintended effects (Hazy and Silberstang 2009). Thus, complex systems interactions keep changing, which makes the theory a perfect fit for the ever-changing organizations as well as the hypercomplex network of global societies (Anderson 1999; Bird 2011). Sargut and McGrath (2011) found that there are three properties of complex organizational environments:

1. Multiplicity (the number of potentially interacting elements)
2. Interdependence (how connected those elements are)
3. Diversity (the degree of heterogeneity)

Sargut and McGrath further argued that the greater the multiplicity, interdependences, and diversity, the greater the complexity. However, Cardwell (2005) believed there are good reasons for complexity, even though most organizational leaders would have preferred dealing with simple issues in decision-making.

The complexity of contemporary organizations makes it difficult to predict what will happen in organizations, because systems interact in unexpected ways (Cardwell 2005; Sargut and McGrath 2011). Furthermore, Sargut and McGrath argued the following:

(a) It is quite difficult to make sense of things/people.
(b) The degree of complexity could be beyond cognitive limits.
(c) It is harder to place bets: past behavior may not predict its future behavior.
(d) The outlier may often be more significant than the average.
(e) Analytic leadership tools are inadequate.

The enlisted factors above testify to the complexity of contemporary organizational leadership and the apparent ignorance in some of the complex concepts.

## Challenges of Complex Systems

Many reasons account for the challenges of adapting to complex organizational leadership systems, including unexpected consequences, unexpressed emotions, assumptions, making sense of the situation, and bad followership (Kellerman 2004; Sargut and McGrath 2011). Even in organizations engaged in continuous learning (Daft 2009), fundamental issues of how formal and tacit learning could be dispersed throughout the organization. Who is involved in the organizational learning? Where does it take place? What is learned? How it could be applied to the organizational situation remains unresolved (Easterby-Smith, Crossan, and Nicolini 2000; Mumford 2006; Senge 2006).

## Possible Solutions to the Complex System

A perfect blend of natural- or life-science and social-science concepts of leadership theories in a recreated equilibrium could be a solution to the challenges of complex systems (van Vugt 2011). Further, an integrated leadership theory would not only make leadership studies quite simple but actually interesting for both the social- and natural-science communities. Moreover, an integrated leadership theory could lead to leadership practitioners accepting, appreciating, adjusting, and adapting natural sciences into social sciences' leadership theories to possibly answer the following questions of what historical changes have taken place in the leader-follower relationship? And, what is the nature of bad leadership (Kellerman 2004)?

Additionally, smart tradeoff decisions could be embedded in models of complex theories to make both leaders and followers better able to innovate, collaborate, and connect with one another in an integrated approach. Again, a conscious attempt at understanding underlying assumptions of an individual's behavior could create empathetic thinking in complex leadership situations (Anderson 1999; Chan 2005). However, ethical ambivalences add to the complexities (Cuila 2001). There seems to be simultaneous and contradictory attitudes and feelings in organizational leadership, as well as continual fluctuations between competing duties, colliding contradictions, and imperfect options (Cuilla 2001; Price 2006). Uncertainty as to which approach or system to follow also abounds in organizations. It should be stated that the individual leaders, followers, organizations, stakeholders, community, country, and even the global environment add to the complexity (Easterby-Smith et al. 2000; Bird and Osland 2004). There is much to be gleaned from analysis of a leader's awareness and understanding of the following:

(a) Personal identity ("Who am I?")
(b) Personal role ("Who do I represent?")

(c) Personal responsibility ("What is expected of me could create a sense of self-awareness in dealing with the ethical ambivalences." (Cuilla 2001; Johnson 2007)

A common understanding from integrated concepts could also solve the complex leadership situations as well as dealing with a common understanding of each scientific domain.

## The 4A Concept

It is imperative, from the ongoing discussion, for life science and social science to *accept, appreciate, adjust, and adapt* to each other by picking the common constructs of each theory to build on each other's strengths. Four steps are recommended in the 4A concept include Step 1 (Inspire), Step 2 (Discover), Step 3 (Training), and Step 4 (Apply).

## Step 1: Inspire

Proponents of natural science and social science should first accept that each approach adds to the body of leadership knowledge. Thus, contemporary leadership theorists can link natural-science and social-science experiences to the central concept of working hand in hand in identification and design of a unified leadership concept that is relevant to modern-day leadership challenges.

This will inspire and help leadership students to understand why an integrated natural science/social science leadership study is relevant.

## Step 2: Discover

The integrated natural science/social science studies will help leadership practitioners and researchers to provide stakeholders with the relevant information needed to appreciate each other's worldview. This will lay central concepts of each concept bare. Such information should include all facts the natural scientists and social scientists know about leadership, norms, settings, traditions, history, and geographical details, as well as possible areas of conflict.

This will help leadership students to understand what they need to know about both schools of thought of leadership.

## Step 3: Training

The adjustment to new ideas of an integrated natural science/social science leadership study needs training and continuous learning. Leadership researchers and institutions should provide curious minds with opportunities and tools to explore and practice new information, theories, suggestions, and even fears of the information given in Step 2. This is a critical step; information alone is not enough to adjust to new learning and a new worldview.

Using Step 3, researchers should help the leadership community address the issue of how integrated natural science and social science concepts can be applied.

## Step 4: Apply

In Step 4, researchers and practitioners can encourage students and followers to adapt to the new natural science/social science models of leadership. They should invite people from these two different perspectives (natural scientists and social scientists) to make life responses to the new ideas of each model of leadership studies. This step will provide students and followers in organizations with opportunities for creative self-expression and exploration of knowledge.

All such activities would help students to address what steps need to be taken to ensure change when all the facts and information are laid bare in each concept of leadership studies. This way, leadership researchers and practitioners can appeal to most students and followers in organizations: those who enjoy talking about their peculiar knowledge and problems, those who need more information of other leadership concepts, those who want to know how it all fits into their beliefs and values, and those who want to apply the new integrated knowledge to change.

## Conclusion

Contemporary, complex organizational systems have created—and continue to create—many ignorant spots in organizational leadership. Competing leadership theories, philosophical contradictions, overly normative and ideological focus, overly humanistic approach (Hannah et al. 2014), and specialization in learning further widens the divide gap. Leadership is about influence (Northouse 2010; Bass and Bass 2008), and the only way to expand knowledge and effective influence of leaders and leadership studies is through an integrated study and practice.

# CHAPTER 2

## PHILOSOPHICAL AND DEFINITIONAL GAPS IN LEADERSHIP

If leaders are prepared to be flexible, keep an open mind, and commit to continuous learning, they will grow richer in knowledge and wisdom, despite changes and bumps in their work. Researchers and practitioners understand this concept. However, definitional dissimilarities could disturb the profession, instead of portraying a rewarding and great experience. Some of the definitions share common ideas, while others appear to have a completely different perspective. As an example, Day (2000) defined leadership as an integral part of a group process. Bass and Bass (2008) claimed that leadership in an organization is determined by legitimate principles and norms of the structure within which leadership occurs. Zaccaro and Klimoski (2001) contended that organizational purpose should be the direction of leaders seeking a collective approach with followers to complete a given task within a legally structured entity.

On the other hand, Greenleaf (1998) considered leadership as a process of serving others as servants. Yet, Dunoon (2008) maintained that leadership entails influence grounded in continuous learning that is highly relational and process focused. However, Northouse (2010) defined leadership as a process whereby an individual influences a group of individuals to achieve a common goal. Northouse's definition brings four important leadership philosophies to light:

(a) Process of how the leader affects and is affected by followers
(b) Influencing factor of how the leader affects followers positively
(c) Leadership taking place in a context of groups

17

(d) Directing followers' energies to achieve a common goal

Evidently, other definitions above have different philosophical underpinnings. Since leadership also occurs in groups, there could be no leader without followers (Northouse 2010). Therefore, a leader with no followers is just hallucinating. Thus, the expectation of leadership appears to be positive influence, service, continuous learning, and relationship building. The leader is involved in the interpersonal influence, uses his or her influence to direct organizational goals, and articulates a vision that followers are inspired to follow (Canabou and Overholt 2001). Unfortunately, not all the definitions capture these important concepts. Definitional variations are not the only challenge. There are theoretical variations as well.

## Theoretical Foundations of Leadership

Many theories of leadership abound in organizations. According to Bryman (2006), organizational researchers and designers have to use theories to predict and verify whether results correspond to what was predicted. In a related study, Nahavandi (2009) conceptualized that the history of modern leadership theories has three eras:

(a) The trait era (ranging from the 800s to the mid-1940s, when it was believed that leaders were born)
(b) The behavioral era (mid-1940s to early 1970s, when leadership studies focused on behaviors, because the trait approach did not yield expected results)
(c) The contingency era (ranging from the early 1960s to present, which appears to succeed in explaining the multifaceted aspects of leadership)

According to Nahavandi (2009), more than forty years of the trait study provided little evidence to justify the assertion that leaders are born. It appeared that behaviors could be observed more objectively, measured more precisely, or taught more easily than traits (Nahavandi 2009; Northouse 2010).

However, the contingency theory appears to provide a comprehensive approach to understanding contemporary leadership (Nahavandi 2009; Northouse 2010). Specifically, situational factors are taken into consideration in contingency theories, thereby making leadership inherently situational (Northouse 2010; Bird 2011; Cuilla 2012). Although the contingency approach to leadership studies continues to be well accepted, the most recent approaches appear to focus on relationships between leaders and followers and on various aspects of charismatic and visionary leadership (Nahavandi 2009; Northouse 2010). The most important theoretical question is whether the focus will continue to shift or not.

The purpose of this chapter was to assess conceptual themes of seven leadership theories—Authenticity Theory, Change, Innovation and Entrepreneurship Theory, Organizational Learning Theory, Globalization and Multiculturalism Theory, Governance and Ethics Theory, Servant Leadership Theory, and Organizational Theory and Research—to determine common themes and anticipate future shifts. These theories were purposefully selected because they guide leaders and organizations to produce replicable experiments in a given organizational phenomenon (Bryman 2006). Other leadership theories include Contingency Theory, Transactional and Transformational Theories, and Complex Leadership Theory. The concepts of servant as a leader, change, innovation and entrepreneurship, and ethics and governance runs through this analysis to prove a philosophical point and to demonstrate scholarship and leadership practices in organizations. It begins with the worldview of the author.

## Worldview and Personal Leadership

The personal philosophy of the author is a worldview built on lifelong learning, travels, experience in leading international and community organizations, and wisdom acquired through long years of education. The term "worldview" was coined by a German, Karl Jasper, in the nineteenth century. Jasper's original *weltancshauug* volume describes frames of references in which the mental life of an individual takes place. These frame of references or *weltancshauug* could be objective or subjective (Stuckard 2003). The subjective piece discusses frames of reference as attitudes or *eistellungen,* while the objective piece defines the frame under world pictures. Tweed (2002) believed attitudes are formal patterns and structures of mental existence in which one experiences the world actively, contemplatively, or rationally. Thus, innate ideas expressed in the leadership philosophy are rational, objective, and active frames in which the author sees the world of leadership.

## Purpose of Worldview in Leadership

Working knowledge of one's worldview provides a pattern of adapting beliefs and values to the work environment, working with followers as a team, and understanding each individual's perspective at work (Naugle 2002). A personal understanding of worldview also guides understanding of different worldviews in leadership studies and at the workplace. Thus, the author argues that a leader's worldview is just one aspect of the many worldviews at the workplace. Imposing a personal worldview on others could affect organizational success, because individuals see issues from different perspectives (Naugle 2002). Furthermore, understanding one's worldview could join the abstract with the concrete at the workplace (Bellman 2002). The congruence of ensuring that words and behavior are of one spirit not only promotes integrity, it also places service to followers as the single-minded purpose of leadership (Bellman 2002).

This single-minded approach appears to join the abstract with the concrete through personal and shared experiences and understanding, which inform an individual's worldview (Bellman 2002). Thus, worldview could be a product of a personal experience, intuition, or teachings one has sought in a quest for understanding

(Harrison 2010). According to Bellman (2002), it is one thing for a leader to see a problem clearly and another to act on it successfully. How leaders practice their personal worldviews at the workplace, as well as accept followers' worldview, could determine their effectiveness or lack thereof at the workplace. The answer appears to lie in empathetic thinking. The essentially logical belief is that if leaders could help followers live out their own vision, through that process, the leader has learned to live out hers or his (Bellman 2002). Thus, the act of living out one's own vision and implementing a collective vision and purpose in a given situation is how the abstract evolves into concrete meaning for followers (Bellman 2002). When the abstract becomes concrete, calling comes to light.

## Calling

Calling appears to originate from personal stories (Novak 1996). According to Novak, calling is a unique and valuable mission because it is an opportunity for unvarnished expression of the integrity and spirituality of the individual. An individual's words, actions, and identity could be a living philosophy of an individual's calling (Novak 1996). In my case, I grew up in a poor family, raised by an illiterate and unemployed single mother. At the age of fourteen, mother called one evening and said, "Son, you are the oldest of five kids. Today, I declare you a son, father, and husband. If you fail us, we all die."

Leadership was entrusted to me from that day. I worked hard to pay school fees, as well as the fees for siblings, and put food on the table. Today, I hold a doctorate, and all my siblings are doing well in life. Basically, the humble beginning and the reality of either being responsible or seeing the whole family perish at a tender age has given me a personal identity and a calling to serve. The service spirit has seen him as a leader from high school, college, community, and many organizations, both local and international. Novak (1996) stated that callings are like that.

According to Novak (1996), two things are normally required in a calling: the God-given ability to do the job, and the equally God-given enjoyment in doing it because of a desire to do it. The author enjoys serving others, and they in turn, accept his services. There is a personal, inward satisfaction for helping others, especially those who cannot pay anything back in return. The author's dream is to serve his country through education and awareness creation, and he encourages readers to also serve from their hearts. Calling is fulfilled through personal values.

## Values

In traditional societies, there is an ancient, well-respected, and sacred traditional value. According to customs, leaders do not infringe on the privacy of individuals, because it is not their business to do so. Outspokenness, often in the form of damaging disclosures, could be a traditional violation. However, with increased knowledge and travels, and learning and growth, the author has observed that the range of ethical expectations for leaders spans a wide area of professional and moral standards. Without ethical values, a leader will not succeed. Even if she manages to succeed, lack of values will bring her down. Thus, ethical values are the flagship of leadership. The term *ethics* refers to a system of moral values or principles intended to govern organizational leadership conduct (Price 2006).

According to Cuilla (2012), knowledge could both be a problem and a solution. Cuilla further argued that before leaders embark on any organizational endeavor, they should ask the following questions:

(a) Am I doing the right thing?
(b) Am I doing it the right way?
(c) Am I doing it for the right reason?
(d) Am I using what I have learned?

Thus, doing the right thing, the right way, and for the right reasons, based on existing knowledge and experience, is an espoused personal and professional value of leadership. Kant's (1964) moral principle of categorical imperative guides personal leadership practices. Specifically, the principle stipulates that anything that is considered inappropriate must be inappropriate at all times. Conversely, right is right and should be upheld at all times and for all. This is a personal value that also guides the "sharpen the saw" (Covey 2015) leadership concept with a spiritual piece that encourages leaders to take care of themselves.

## Spiritual Formation in Leadership

The concept known as "sharpening the saw" means leaders must take personal care of self (Covey 2015). Taking care of self through exercise, reading, and meditation are constructs of sharpening one's saw, or else it goes blunt. Meditation and spending time with nature are the spiritual piece of spiritual formation in leadership (Covey 2015). Harrison (2010) defined spirituality as wholeness emanating from both inner and outer lives that enrich each other when brought together. Daily meditation and reading of faith-based materials bonds the inner and the outer selves of the leader together. Therefore, spirituality is not a private issue in leadership, but public as well, because it influences both the leader's worldview as well as his values (Boa 2001; Lambert 2009; Harrison 2010).

According to Lambert (2009), contemporary discussions of workplace spirituality all claim that one could serve others, be truly deeply spiritual, and derive wealth all at the same time. Lambert further argued that leading a business could be a path to spiritual growth, a means to creating a better world, and a path to prosperity. Thus, spirituality at the workplace does not take anything away from the leader; rather, it fulfills her in creating a better world. Therefore, leaders and followers must be encouraged to bring their spirituality and spiritual practices into the workplace (Harrison 2010). It takes nothing away from productivity and effectiveness.

Harrison (2010) posited that people are becoming more open about their beliefs and practices in working with things unseen. However, Harrison found that most people in organizations have come to identify the principle of religious and spiritual freedom with a prohibition against speaking publicly about what individuals do and think in their spiritual lives. Nevertheless, a leader's spiritual life must involve her spiritual values, myths, visions, ideas, images, and emotions that make up her sense of what it means to be a leader of an organization (Lambert 2009; Harrison 2010). Whatever one's preferred way of connecting with the spirit, spirituality at the workplace should be encouraged by leaders in organizations through meditation, prayer, ceremony, rituals, or simply through inquiry of the heart (Harrison 2010). The point here is simple: spirituality is personal, and you cannot have that person at work leaving his spirituality at home.

## Personal Leadership Analysis

As narrated in over two million books of personal stories and profiles of leadership studies and practices, the profession of leadership seems to be embedded in the story of positive organizational outcome (van Vugt and Ahuja 2011). This profession that often feels more like a family than just an assembly of people epitomizes the emblematic spirit of influence on followers (Northouse 2010). Here, the calling is neither shouted from the rooftop nor proclaimed through officialdom in egoistic thoughts or greater rewards. Rather, leadership is a calling to change followers' lives and make them co-leaders. Changing followers' lives could be championed in an organizational mission that gives every single follower the opportunity to achieve intellectual and personal development (Bass and Bass 2008). Intellectual and personal development could also be achieved by adding value to the organizational atmosphere through diversity and cultural understanding of followers' immediate and global environment (Schein 2010; Bird 2011).

However, traditional ways of leadership have not adequately matched the reality of organizational outcome; the devil lies in the detail of complex and unpredictable organizational environment (Bass and Bass 2008; Northouse 2010; Bird 2011). Therefore, contemporary leadership studies must be grounded in total quality of continuous learning and access to developmental tools that are relevant to followers' needs, constant innovation in daily interactions, and integration of each follower in the learning process (Senge 1990). It is not enough for the leader to show up in an organization and explain a sequence of actions, direct operations, strategize an operational plan, or control proceedings at a meeting. Rather, it is the daily diligence to see to it that each follower with an unsure path leaves the workplace with a value, purpose, and aspiration to contribute to the common good of society (Boa 2001).

The star of the organization is not the leader. The stars are followers. It is about them, not the leader. Therefore, the leader's role is to facilitate followers' stardom by authentically engaging them in learning, personal development, change processes, spiritual growth, services, stewardship, accountability, and innovation for effective outcome. This process could create citizenship, comradeship, community, and a path of nurturing co-leaders (Northouse 2010). The leader may not be recognized in the final outcome, but a positive difference could be made with an indelible mark on the wall. The indelible marks

ents they share, or memories they
o longer at the workplace. It might
not been for Mrs. Smith, I wouldn't
onal human resources exams," or
n a difficult family situation saved
effective leadership are in adding
ect; and involving followers in the
portantly, leaders who care appear
reenleaf 1991). In the end, a leader

must train followers to a level where they can do exactly what the leader does at the workplace in her absence.

## Workplace in Retrospect

Most employees appear to struggle in their daily lives with no family support or spiritual propriety (Boa 2001; Lambert 2009). Specifically, the foundations of how to live a spiritual life—an emphasis on family, hard work, a belief in one's distinctive capabilities, being true to self, making informed decisions, and giving back to the community—could be lacking in many individuals. Leadership that does not nurture these common standards might be flawed in meeting followers' immediate and future needs. Therefore, leaders should give followers the best of opportunities to learn to be responsible to themselves, as well as their families, friends, community, and country. Furthermore, leaders must guide followers to work hard for a decent living, believe in one's unique capabilities to make a difference, and to recognize individuals' strengths and weaknesses as well as how to improve upon one's strengths (Bass and Bass 2008). The old status quo of emphasizing on followers' weaknesses should pave way for reinforcing followers' strengths (Cuilla 2012). Daily communication and feedback must also provide critical thinking and reflective skills for followers to explore options and make informed decisions with a perfect understanding that giving back to the community is a moral duty and the right thing to do (Kant 1964).

## Constant Innovation in Workplace Interactions

Constant innovation at the workplace springs from continuous learning, growth, and personal development (Senge 1990). Technology, visualization, role play, dyadic presentations, group work, and meaningful engagement of followers' in questioning, critiquing, answering, and discussing progress are some of the tools in ensuring innovation at the workplace (Senge 1990; Bass and Bass

2008). Leading an organization of a diverse nature requires constant innovation in asking appropriate questions, creating enriching workplace interactions, and paying attention to each follower's reactions, either implied or explicit (Bass and Bass 2008; Schein 2010). Providing the right direction and being mindful to respect each follower could lead to a clanlike work environment and enhance positive organizational outcome (Daft 2007; Bass and Bass 2008).

## Integrating Followers in the Learning Process

A follower's effective cooperation in organizational processes and activities depends on how the leader impacts her environment with a leadership style that creates mutual understanding (Cuilla 2012). The leader's constant emphasis on the soft skills—a good work ethic, empathy, responsibility, and dignity—enhances followers' cooperation with the leader (Cuilla 2012). According to Chaleff (2012), leaders and followers share a common purpose because followers also assume responsibilities of initiating improvements, supporting leaders energetically, participating in transforming the organization, and taking a moral stand when needed. This process is both an art and a science (Nahavandi 2009). It is science because the process is systematic in studying followers' behavior between ends and means of an organizational objective. It is also an art because the leader has the flexibility to dream by adapting to the moment and sharing ideas with followers to enrich the organizational experience (Nahavandi 2009). An effective blend of the art and science of leadership creates a positive impact in followers' minds to continue to grow in wisdom and knowledge and to generate positive organizational outcomes. Thus, the leader must create organizational learning processes that are open, conducive, and collaborative to create positive organizational outcome (Senge 1990).

## Organizational System

According to Daft (2008), formal systems are implemented in organizations to manage the growing amount of complex information and to detect variations from established standards and goals. Organizations, as learning enterprises, rely on formal systems to respond to competition, make efficient use of resources, and cope with the dynamic and complex environmental changes (Senge 1990; Daft 2009). Therefore, leaders should adopt a natural system of horizontal structure, empowered roles, shared information, collaborative strategy, and adaptive culture to support effective organizational outcomes (Hurst 1995). Hurst's natural design system aims to improve a leader's productivity and the quality of followers' learning. The system consists of opt-in instead of opt-out approaches to decision making, transparent evaluations, and an additional informal system of policy implementations (Senge 1994). Thus, positive organizational outcome is not a rounded vision of big ideas (Papert 2000). Rather, it is the daily infinite details of engaging and inspiring followers. It is the culture, environment, technology, goals, and strategy carefully woven for professional organizational learning environments that lead to effective leadership and followership. It is the daily motivation, good relationships, and personal connections that radiate authentic and exemplary leadership relevant to followers' needs. This idea bears fruit if the leader is ready to be a servant.

## Servant as a Leader

Servant leadership, as developed by Robert Greenleaf, emphasized the belief that before one can be an effective leader, she must be willing to serve others (Greenleaf 1977, 13). Greenleaf argued that the servant leader is servant first who begins with the natural feeling that one wants to serve. Thereafter, a conscious choice brings one to aspire to lead. Thus, the concept of servant leadership focus on team work and leaders inspiring followers to achieve a common goal. Servant leaders place the needs of followers above their own personal needs, with a thought that once each individual flourishes, so will the community (Greenleaf 1991).

Spears (2002) posited that the quest for organizational leadership is a rekindled spirit of sacrifice and selfless devotion to causes greater than the leader. Drucker (1996) seems to support this concept when he suggested that great leaders are not only bred from great causes; leaders, at their best, also breed great causes. Since being a leader in one context does not guarantee leadership skills in every other kind of situation, effective leadership begins with a personal commitment to spiritual propriety, which provides foundational gift of all leadership (Boa 2001; Lambert 2009). Basically, leadership requires loving followers and stakeholders of an organization (Boa 2001), because followers relate better with leaders who identify with their needs and problems (Boa 2001; Lambert 2009). Thus, a leader focusing on nurturing spiritual growth in service by helping followers meet unmet needs could develop a positive atmosphere for effective organizational outcomes. It is difficult to lead people who feel unloved. On the other hand, it is much easier to lead followers who sense and feel the leader's genuine love (Boa 2001).

Effective leaders give more than what is expected of them at the workplace. They build a community to an extent that the absence of every employee is missed by others. They motivate followers with a personal belief to succeed. Leaders should be open-minded in serving followers. Greenleaf (1991) argued that an essential component of service is to be available, share leadership skills, and empower followers to develop other significant leadership skills. This begins with leaders and followers discovering and evaluating strengths and weaknesses together, in order to build on each other's strengths (Bass and Bass 2008). The next concept is that individuals are not called to be leaders but servers who maintain courageous convictions (Spears 2002). Colin Powell (1995) found that the day soldiers stop bringing leaders their problems is the day leaders stopped leading them. Here, Powell's argument is that leaders will never stop solving problems. Strong conviction with a desire to solve problems must hold leaders up when the enormous nature of problems is ready to hold leaders down. On a good day, the strong conviction that holds leaders up must also hold the organization in building a familylike community (Daft 2009).

However, the challenge facing many organizations is simply and squarely a failure of wise leadership (Sternberg 2007). Many organizational problems stem from the inability of leaders to rise to the responsibility of leadership, as well as the challenge of personal example, which are the hallmarks of true leadership (Greenleaf 1991, Daddieh 2009). As an organization of one purpose, vision, and mission, leaders should build a community of employees who are sincere with themselves (both in their private and professional lives) and are committed to each other's success (Boa 2001, Lambert 2009). If leaders are wrong, they should admit it. If followers are right, leaders should encourage and motivate them. The motivation should be strategic, linking actions to outcomes. Leaders should also create a cordial atmosphere where followers can freely express their opinions on organizational issues of common interest and importance. Leaders should not seek empty and hollow honor, but serve with accepted basis, humility, and be the first to serve others (Greenleaf 1991). Coffen (2009) rightly argued that achievements are soon forgotten and awards tarnish. Accolades and certificates fade and get filed. Those who make differences in organizations appear not to be the ones with the most credentials, fame, or awards. They are those who care. Therefore, servant leaders are those who care.

## Spears's Ten Characteristics of Servant Leadership

Greenleaf (1991) stated that the best test of servant leadership is in analyzing if those served by the leader grow as individuals. Do they, while being served, become healthier, wiser, freer, more autonomous, and more likely themselves to become servants? According to Greenleaf (1991), if the answers to these questions are *yes*, then the leader is a servant leader. Based on Greenleaf's (1991) ideology, Spears (2002) conceptualized ten characteristics of a servant leader:

1) **Listening:** The servant leader must listen to verbal and nonverbal signals and interpret what followers are saying. Additionally, the servant leader must listen to inner thoughts

and feelings and interpret them in daily relations with followers.

2) **Empathy:** Empathetic listeners are the most successful servant leaders.

3) **Healing:** Servant leaders take the opportunity to make whole those with whom they come in contact.

4) **Awareness:** Servant leaders view most situations from a more integrated, holistic position.

5) **Persuasion:** The servant leader should rely on persuasion and decentralized decision making, rather than personal authority and centralized decision making.

6) **Conceptualization:** Servant leaders have the ability to look at a problem or an organization from a conceptualizing perspective or beyond day-to-day realities.

7) **Foresight:** They learn lessons from the past, realities of the present, and likely consequence of a decision for the future.

8) **Stewardship:** Leaders commit to serve the needs of others. They also emphasize openness and persuasion.

9) **Commitment to the Growth of People:** Servant leaders have a deep commitment to each individual in an organization.

10) **Building Community:** A servant leader should seek to identify some means for building community among those who work within a given institution.

Spears (2002) argued that servant leaders seek to nurture their abilities to dream great dreams and look at a problem from a conceptual perspective. Therefore, servant leaders are not only focused on the bottom line of their organizations, but they also understand concepts of employee and stakeholder behaviors and needs. They also well work to improve the well-being of both groups (Spears 2002). It is important for the servant as a leader in an organization to lead by example, create an environment where followers would always want to come back to work, respect followers, and create a conducive atmosphere where each employee will genuinely miss work anytime he or she is not working. This could be possible where the leader's selfless examples always give followers something to come back for. The theory of servant leadership also advocates a worldview that the only justification for being in leadership is to provide access, protection, fairness, justice, and the right environment for employees to thrive (Greenleaf 1991). Again, servant leadership theory encourages leaders to use the resources of the organization to improve the standard of living of employees and the community (Spears 2002). Thus, the servant as a leader builds followers up to achieve something they never thought of.

Greenleaf (1991) found that the servant leader exhibits a skill of empathy and sense of awareness for what is occurring around him. Consequently, the servant leader must have a "sense of the unknowable to be able to foresee the unforeseeable" (Greenleaf 1977, 21). Thus, foresight is an important piece of servant leadership because it guides both leaders and followers to plan strategically to achieve organizational goals (Greenleaf 1977; Spears 2002). Spears (2002) conceptualized that foresight allows the servant leader to address and alleviate followers' fears. Therefore, when follower fears are alleviated, trust is built, which strengthens the bond between the leader and followers, allowing for difficult issues to be addressed in good faith (Spears 2002). Building such trust begins with personal authenticity.

## Personal Authenticity

According to Bass and Bass (2008), authentic leadership was identified earlier in transformational leadership research but never fully articulated until recently. Northouse (2010) found that background to the theoretical approach of authenticity research is recent, with the first article appearing in 2003. Even though the concept of personal authenticity is identified from many parameters, Chan (2005) sharpened the definitional focus from three viewpoints:

(a) *Intrapersonal perspective* focuses on the leader and what goes on in the leader.
(b) *Developmental perspective* views leadership as something that could be nurtured in a leader.

(c) *Interpersonal relationship* emphasizes relationship created by both leaders and followers together.

However, Chang (2005) critiqued some aspects of authentic leadership, including self-knowledge, and argued for aspirational approach to authenticity that is best pursued under conditions of the rarely noted virtue of humility. Chang posited that the zeitgeist of the early 2000s has been characterized by a loss of trust in many organizations, including corporate and political leadership. A concomitant desire for more simple, transparent, and trustworthy leadership style seems more appropriate in contemporary leadership (Taylor 2004). Personal authenticity is viewed from the practical approach of George's (2003) characteristics of authentic leaders. George found that authentic leaders have a genuine desire to serve others, know themselves, and feel free to lead from their core values. George further specified five basic characteristics of authentic leaders:

(a) They understand their purpose.
(b) They have strong values about the right thing to do.
(c) They establish trusting relationships with others.
(d) They demonstrate self-discipline and act on their values.
(e) They are passionate about their mission by acting from the heart.

Practically, an authentic leader holds personal values in high esteem and exhibits a strong sense of purpose. The authentic leader also understands that her private life is not detached from her public life, but both are interrelated in building her behavior (Boa 2001). Authenticity must be the leader's social purpose, the foundation of her approach to responsible business, and a shining spotlight of a deep connection between organizational strategy and responsibility (Chan 2005).

The premise is that being authentic is fundamental in building trust, comradeship, and foundations of organizational success. Therefore, the legacy of authenticity is a reputation of building and maintaining trust, an essential ingredient for organizational success. According to Galford and Drapeau (2003), shareholders, customers, employees, suppliers, and communities have high expectations of authenticity in leaders and employees. Galford and Drapeau conceptualized that the only way to welcome those expectations and live up to them is for leaders to be authentic in words and actions. An important component that nurtures authenticity is the way leaders manage their responsibility to their families and in the communities in which they work. For instance, leaders should develop authentic and ethical frameworks that set out major elements of making decisions and being accountable for one's actions. This thought, again, makes authenticity an individual issue (George 2003). Therefore, the individual should be encouraged to focus on self-assessment to know personal strengths and weaknesses, as well as where the individual believes she has a unique role to play in the organization (Valk 2009). Additionally, leaders should encourage an agenda of responsible business activities that cover a range of disciplines from personal relationships to spirituality and diversity policies to build personal authenticity at the workplace. The building of personal authenticity leads to group authenticity. Moreover, leaders should recognize that any definition of responsible business that promotes personal authenticity is built on and contributes to the organization's culture, values, and behavior. To conclude, authentic behaviors that contribute positively to organizational success should be rewarded, with the intent to encourage employees to do more. Success in organizations rests on the shoulders of employees. Therefore, leaders should submit to employee needs and encourage individual authenticity, because changing individuals changes the organization.

## Organizational Theory and Research

Organizational theories and research guide leaders' knowledge in past, present, and future phenomena (Fielding and Gilbert 2006). According to Coombs (2004), theories and research provide empirical evidence of events, patterns, and ideas in building leaders' quality initiatives, efficiency, and effectiveness in organizations. Theories also solve puzzles in organizations and explain organizational occurrence (Fielding and Gilbert 2006). Thus, leaders should ensure that specific theories fit into predicting an organizational outcome as well as verify whether the outcome corresponds with what was predicted or not. Tosi (2009) found that organizational theories and research could provide accurate predictions of events. Thus, the strength of a theory is an effective tool for predicting organizational outcomes. Theories also appear to help organizations to coordinate activities and events as well as make effective decisions (Coombs 2004). It appears that most leaders lack the appropriate theoretical skills to create an effective organizational learning environment (Daft 2009). Therefore, continuous learning of organizational theories and research should be a shared organizational purpose in binding theory and leadership together to serve as a key for leaders to act responsibly within a given theoretical framework.

Furthermore, theories help leaders analyze and diagnose organizational issues for informed decisions of the system, design, culture, and outcomes (Cameron and Quinn 2006). Thus, theories guide leaders to use modern information technologies to adapt and influence changing environment, add value, accommodate diversity, and promote good work ethics (Daft 2009). For instance, theoretical models and assessment tools could help leaders reform and review policies to improve effectiveness and create a family-like organization that links theories to the business foundation as well as use key differentiators as a path to organizational success (Daft 2009).

Moreover, leaders could learn from covenant-building, theoretical processes to build unquestioning relations in organizations and explain to followers the higher purpose of the organization in the relation-building process (Gunderman 2011). This is possible if leaders know how to treat employees well (Kevany 2008). When leaders treat followers as though they are building a relationship for a lifetime, the followers are committed to work and personal development that could manifest in the organization's activities and programs

(Pirie and McCuddy 2007). It then becomes possible to build a covenantlike theory of comradeship at the workplace (Gunderman 2011). Thus, building quality theoretical initiatives and efficiencies and maximizing employee strengths in day-to-day operations must be embedded in leadership theories for organizational practices, stories, successes, and effective outcomes (Bass and Bass 2008).

## Ethics and Governance

Ethics in leadership has been long on words but short on tools and personal examples. In an exploratory research designed to understand what the term "ethical leadership" means, Brown and Trevino (2006) argued that ethical leaders ought to be honest and trustworthy. However, there seems to be inadequate practical guidance as to how a leader must behave in an "honest and trustworthy" manner (Badaracco 2002). The question here is that if a leader flip-flops, does that inconvenience honesty and trustworthiness? According to Price (2006), ethics is a branch of philosophy that explores the nature of moral virtue and evaluates human actions in terms of right or wrong. Brown and Trevino (2006) established that philosophical ethics, also known as moral philosophy, seeks to conduct the study of morality through rational outlook grounded in notions of human happiness or well-being. Thus, ethical philosophy adopts methods that determine whether an action is morally *good* or *bad* or *right* or *wrong* (Brown and Trevino 2006; Price 2006).

Corporate governance, on the other hand, is defined as a system that is used by organizations to control and direct their operations and the operations of employees (Stanwick and Stanwick 2009). According to Stanwick and Stanwick, the board of directors plays roles based on the belief that the actions of the board represent goals and objectives of stakeholders. Thus, the board should be positive, certifying, engaged, intervening, and operational. They further argued that CEOs' compensation and the financial performance of an organization had no direct relationship. This finding is quite debatable, judging from the current perception that most CEOs are overpaid (according to their salary ratio with employee wages). Besides, organizational governance means corporate compliance with the law, code of ethics, internal control management, risk-management programs, test controls, and frequent audits (Stanwick and Stanwick 2009). Thus, leaders in corporate governance must eschew corruption, extortion, and embezzlement to satisfy the mandate of governance entrusted into their hands.

A deontological approach to ethics also seems appropriate for ethics and governance in organizational leadership, with a consistent thought that actions have intrinsic moral value (Kant 1964). For instance, leadership actions such as keeping promises, telling the truth, and respecting followers' rights are considered inherently good, while leadership actions such as intimidation, manipulation, or lying are deemed inherently bad (Kant 1964; Brown and Trevino 2003). Therefore, no matter how much positive outcome one might achieve from lying, the action of lying will never be right (Kant 1964). People who put themselves in leadership roles should be held to a higher standard. Good morals and higher ethical standards must be the yardstick used when choosing a leader, because leaders become role models that followers look up to (Cuilla 2005). Furthermore, there should be ethical, legal, and policy requirements in organizations and clear channels for reporting unethical behaviors that are not consistent with organizational philosophy or policy (Johnson 2007). This is in line with Kant's (1964) law of categorical imperative: what is wrong is wrong, no matter who is leading it or is behind it. The opposite is true for what is right. According to Solansky (2008), it is important for a leader to develop internal locus of control in every thought process by being accountable and responsible for an individual leader's actions. Therefore, the leader must also factor accountability into every decision made and realize that if things could be done ethically, it is up to the leader to fulfill professional obligations to the organizational code of conduct and make altruistic moral judgments (Johnson 2007).

## Conclusion

In conclusion, Klann (2007) argued that ethical leaders have the ability to recognize and define ethical dilemmas and to develop plans and strategies for resolving those problems with a clear moral conscience. Leaders are supposed to lead and follow. Therefore, the leader's ability to think ethically enables her to be both a smart leader and a wise follower (Price 2006). A smart leader and a wise follower also appear to embrace change.

## Change, Innovation, and Entrepreneurship

Northouse (2010) defined leadership as a process whereby an individual influences a group of individuals to achieve a common goal. The influencing process could imply a change in activity, system, or procedure or policy in an organization. The leader could also influence followers by communicating her ideas, gaining the acceptance and support of followers, and implementing the ideas with followers through change (Northouse 2010). However, reasons for change could be only the first step in the change process (Burnes 2004). It is actually making the change and getting value from that change that matters. Bird (2011) conceptualized that there are two types of leaders: those frustrated by change and those fascinated by change. Whether a leader is frustrated or fascinated by change, one thing is clear: change is imminent.

In a change model, Schein (2010) found that there are three levels of culture: artifacts, shared values, and basic assumptions. Artifacts are factors such as what is seen and heard in organizations. Artifacts could also be languages or the way people dress in organizations. Shared values are based on what groups within the organization learn about what is acceptable as well as what is unacceptable. Basic assumptions, on the other hand, are the agreed starting point for decision making within the organization. Thus, the basic assumptions are the deeper-level linchpins for the organization and maintenance of ethical culture. Since the basic assumptions are the foundations for the decision-making process, changing culture from the basic assumption level changes individual organizational behavior (Schein 2010). In relation to leadership, Schein proposed two types of mechanisms of change of culture: primary mechanisms and secondary articulation and reinforcement mechanisms. Schein posited that leaders have the ability to use many mechanisms to lead by example, to communicate ethical values to followers, and to implement positive reinforcement to clearly establish what acceptable and desirable behavior in an organization is.

## Entrepreneurship

Longnecker, Petty, and Hoy (2012) conceptualized that entrepreneurs are frequently thought to be individuals who discover market needs and launch new firms to meet those needs. They are risk takers who provide an impetus for change, innovation, and progress in economic life. Thus, an entrepreneur could be a business founder, an owner, franchisee, owner-manager, or a leader in both for-profit and nonprofit organizations (Longnecker et al. 2012). Therefore, leaders as entrepreneurs pursue opportunities in either a new or existing organizations, create value, assume risk, and get rewarded for their efforts.

## Theoretical Foundations of Change

Kotter and Cohen's (2002) *eight-step change process*, Lewin's (1947) *unfreeze, change, and re-freeze*, and Schein's (2010) *changing culture changes individuals* are few of the theoretical foundations of change models. As an example, Kotter and Cohen's eight-step change process could be practically used in organizations for the following purposes:

    (a) Increasing urgency in developing, reviewing, or sustaining an organizational policy
    (b) Building a guiding team to create a climate of change
    (c) Getting the vision of policies right

(d) Communicating for a buy-in to engage and enable the whole organization in the policy-change process
(e) Enabling action to create a momentum in practicing the new policy
(f) Creating short-term wins
(g) Not letting up the change
(h) Making change stick by implementing and sustaining the change

Kotter and Cohen's (2002) change process systematically takes organizations through the change process and suggested the following:

(a) Leaders lead change processes by examining the market and competitive realities.
(b) Leaders put together a group with enough power to lead change.
(c) Leaders create a vision to help direct the change effort.
(d) Leaders use every vehicle possible to communicate new vision and strategies.
(e) Leaders get rid of obstacles.
(f) Leaders plan for visible improvements in performance of "wins."
(g) Leaders increase credibility to change all systems, structures, and policies.
(h) Leaders create better performances through better leadership and more effective management.

Kotter (2002) suggested that leaders should show followers truth in the change process to influence their feelings. According to Kotter, the process of *analysis-think-change* is ineffective in the change process, while the process of *see-feel-change* is powerful. Kotter posited that highly successful organizations know how to deal with employee resistance. They know how to grab opportunities and avoid hazards. They see the bigger leaps are associated with winning big, and winning big entails creating a better performance and understanding through better leadership as well as connecting new behaviors to organizational success (Kotter 2002).

In an earlier change study, Lewin (1947) introduced the three-step change process. Lewin's three steps of unfreeze, change, and refreeze highlighted opposing forces that are often at work when leaders introduce a new change initiative to followers. Lewin (1947) referred to a process of confronting existing mental maps and replacing them with new ones as "unfreezing." Lewin (1947) further argued that as a means of challenging the status quo, unfreezing could be accomplished in three ways:

1. Increasing the driving force
2. Decreasing the restraining forces
3. A combination of the two

The second step in the process is changing behavior. The changing process moves the target system or people to a new level of equilibrium. Actions include persuading followers to agree that the new status quo is beneficial to them, while encouraging them to view the problem from a fresh perspective. The third step, refreezing, is to focus on the new approach and new values while institutionalizing the new change. Lewin (1947) conceptualized that the leader should provide more driving forces to overcome existing mental maps of restraining forces before change can be affected and institutionalized.

Schein (2010) advocated that leaders must consider the organizational culture when attempting to understand how to move followers to embrace change. Schein argued that organizational culture, as a concept, points to phenomena that are below the surface that are unconscious. Thus, *culture* is to a *group* what *personality* is to an *individual* (Schein 2004).

Schein (2004, 25) defined culture as "pattern of shared assumptions that was learned by a group as it solved its problems of external adaptation and internal integration that has worked well enough to be considered valid, and therefore, to be taught to new members as the right way to perceive, think, and feel in relation to those problems." According to Schein (2004), many observers analyze culture at the surface or artifact level. This includes the visible products of group—language, style, technology, clothing/manner of dress, emotional displays, myths, and stories about organizations. However, artifacts do not provide deeper source of rituals because they are easy to observe but difficult to decipher (p. 26). The second level, espoused beliefs and values, reflects the original beliefs for the inception of the group or might represent evolved organizational beliefs and values. Schein (2010) argued that to instigate real change innovation, leaders must understand the culture at the deeper or underlying-assumption level. Impacting deeper level thinking entails leaders resurrecting, reexamining, and possibly changing some of the more stable portions of followers' cognitive structure while building relationships for deeper understanding of change. When leaders build relationships with followers in the change process, they better understand how underlying assumptions of change come to life. Anxieties are addressed, and change occurs (Schein 2010).

In organizations, leaders effecting change must define their objectives and constraints, come up with requirements, estimate costs, identify risks and rewards, and measure their influence in the change process. Goals of change should be clearly defined and metrics identified (Northouse 2010). Reasons for change should be identified and captured in a nice, crisp goal statement. The change should also be compatible with the organizational goals and supported by training, tools, and funding to see it through to a logical conclusion of new equilibrium of institutionalized change (Lewin 1947).

## Globalization and Multiculturalism

Every culture in history seems to have, at times, been marginalized, misjudged, or mistreated by personal biases and parochial thinkers (Hall 1973). Yet, these cultures have contributed positively to organizations as well as to the wealth of general knowledge and richness of world culture. As kingdoms have cycled through history, tribes, clans, and groups have made desperate cries to their subjugators not to be maligned, to be seen, appreciated, and not thought less of, but equal with (Hall 1973). In postmodern organizations, diversity has become the "theme du jour" as leaders and organizations recognize that others who may not look, speak, or behave like them could bring value and effectiveness to organizations. Change, uncertainty, and ambiguity are common themes when operating in a global context. Global leaders simply manage accelerating change and differences while simultaneously learning to live in an ambiguous, unfamiliar, or uncomfortable zone that typifies the frustrations and perplexities of working and living in an unknown culture (Antal, Dierkes, and Child 2001).

Bird and Osland (2004) defined global leadership as a process of influencing thinking, attitudes, and behaviors of a global community to work together synergistically to achieve organizational outcome. The comprehensive definition touches on arranging organizational structures and processes, building communities, developing trust, and nurturing a global mind-set to lead change. Bird (2011) compared horizontal and vertical global leadership and drew clear distinction between the two concepts. For instance, vertical leadership seeks to control followers, while horizontal leadership aims to coordinate with followers. Further, vertical leadership believes in knowledge as power; horizontal leadership creates knowledge. Thus, effective global leaders create knowledge and coordinate with followers for effective outcome.

According to Bird (2011), challenges of the twenty-first century would be leveraging differences in global organizations by finding potential leaders to deal with complexities. Bird opined that there are two types of global leaders: those frustrated by differences and those fascinated by differences. Therefore, the social architecture aspects of global leaders' roles involve building an organizational structure with characteristics of entrepreneurship, participation, diversity, trust, collaboration, and innovation, in order to be fascinated by differences at the workplace. Another related concept is the building blocks of global leadership. According to Bird and Osland (2004), threshold traits of integrity, humility, inquisitiveness, and hardiness lead to global knowledge. Bird (2011) further posited the idea of building community that spans beyond boundaries with global training in cognitive dispositions, system thinking, interpersonal skills, and ethical decisions. According to Bird and Osland (2004), the work context of global leaders should be managing multiplicity or multiple stakeholders, ambiguity, and precariousness.

Bird (2011) further argued that global leader problem-solving approaches should be predicated on the following:

(a) Deep domain knowledge
(b) An understanding of the root causes of problems
(c) Attention to cues that others fail to interpret correctly
(d) The use of mental simulation to test possible action steps
(e) An ability to see the big picture
(f) A keen focus on future needs while resolving current issues
(g) An appreciation for a long-term view of situations
(h) The use of personal networks
(i) The importance of building relations
(j) The benefits of bridging intercultural communication gaps
(k) A commitment to engage in mindful dialogue and active listening
(l) Clarity of organizational goals

Bird's (2011) concept of experts and novices also clarified differences between knowledge and beliefs, relevant and irrelevant information, perceived interactions among cues, and how a global leader reacts to nonroutine situations in making decisions under pressure. Bird further posited that the differences between experts and novices could help organizations to identify exceptional global leaders who understands the scope of global work and possesses clear perception of the work content in resolving complex problems through demonstrated intercultural competencies. However, Bird (2012) threw a few caveats into the global leadership discussion:

(a) Not every international experience is equally challenging or leveraged.
(b) There is no way to ensure that each person learns the "right lessons" or develops in the same way in global assignments.
(c) Personal development is personal.

Furthermore, Bird (2011) conceptualized that global is not the issue, complexity is. He demonstrated complexity with an interrelated diversity, ambiguity, and interdependence model in a constant flux and argued that not only are the interdependent forces competing against each other, they are collaborating as well. Thus, Bird encouraged global leaders to learn cause-and-effect interactions and how to filter through the complexity by discovering, architecting, and using systems thinking.

In a related global complexity theory study, Sargut and McGrath (2011) posited that as the global environment becomes more complex, the potential for unintended consequences arises as even small decisions increase. Sargut and McGrath argued that complexity makes it more difficult for global leaders to find a vantage point in responding to global issues. Similarly, Hazy, Goldstein, and Lichtenstein (2007) conceptualized three properties of complex organizational environment:

(a) Multiplicity (the number of potentially interacting elements)
(b) Interdependence (how connected those elements are)
(c) Diversity (the degree of heterogeneity)

Therefore, greater multiplicity, interdependence, or diversity leads to greater complexity in leading global organizations (Hazy et al. 2007).

Global leadership competencies stem from business knowledge of complex systems, intercultural competency, and global organizing expertise (Bird 2011; Sargut and McGrath 2011). Thus, developmental methodologies of planned field trips, individual experiential learning and reflections, learning new values, and a good personal transformation project leads to global leadership competency (Bird and Osland 2004). In another study, Yip (1995) noted that the question is not so much whether companies are in a global industry and have global strategies; it is a matter of degree, and the question becomes how global the industry is and how global the organization's strategy should be. According to Mendenhall et al. (2008), a more horizontal, resource-sharing, coordinating and knowledge-creation leadership promotes globalization and multiculturalism in organizations. The growing importance of world businesses seems to create a strong demand for leaders with international management and leadership skills who are effective at handling global issues.

Adler and Bartholomew (1992) posited that globalization has created the need for leaders to become competent in cross-cultural awareness and practice. Adler and Bartholomew further argued that global leaders need to do the following:

(a) Understand cultural environments worldwide
(b) Learn the perspectives, tastes, trends, and technologies of many other cultures
(c) Be able to work simultaneously with people from many cultures
(d) Adapt to living and communicating in other cultures
(e) Learn to relate to people from other cultures from a position of equality rather than cultural superiority (p. 53).

In a related study, Tichy, Brimm, Charan, and Takeuchi (1992) conceptualized that a global and multicultural leader must have

(a) a global mind-set;

(b) a set of global leadership skills and behaviors;

(c) energy, skills, and talent for global networking;

(d) the ability to build effective multicultural teams; and

(e) global change agent skills.

Thus, a leader trained in global perspective and multiculturalism could be in a better position to handle diversity, nuances, and characteristics of different cultures as well as be sensitive to people in other countries and cultures (Hofstede 2001; Bird and Osland 2004).

A globalized and multicultural leader's personal development requires experiential learning and reflection, crucibles and experiences, extensive practice, challenging cross-cultural exposure, and extracting or absolving traits (Mendenhall et al. 2008). Thus, the globalized and multicultural leader should be attentive to the social environment, interested in continuous learning, ask a lot of questions, observe, and read on global issues to satisfy her curiosity (Kozai Group Inc. 2009). Such a mind-set could lead to multicultural intelligence, which has a positive correlation with multicultural leadership success (Early and Ang 2003). Hofstede's (2001) five cultural dimensions are also an important model in global and multicultural studies:

1) *Power distance* (the extent to which people accept unequal distribution of power)

2) *Uncertainty avoidance* (the extent to which culture tolerates ambiguity)

3) *Individualism* (the extent to which individuals or closely knit social structure, such as the extended family, are the basis of the system)

4) *Masculinity* (the extent to which assertiveness and independence from others is valued)

5) *Time orientation* (the extent to which people focus on past, present, or future)

Hofstede (2001) argued that the combination of these five dimensions lends each national culture its distinctiveness and unique culture. For instance, when compared to forty other nations, the United States was below average on power distance and uncertainty avoidance, highest in individualism, above average on masculinity, and moderate on short-term time orientation.

According to Hofstede, these scores indicate that the United States is a somewhat egalitarian culture in which uncertainty and ambiguity are well tolerated, and a high value is placed on individual achievements, assertiveness, performance, and independence. Sex roles are relatively well defined, and organizations look for quick results with a focus on the present. However, Japan tended to be higher than the United States in power distance, masculinity, and uncertainty avoidance, but considerably lower in individualism, with a long-term orientation because Japan's social structures (family and organizations) are important. Therefore, their power and obedience to them tend to be absolute, risk and uncertainty are averted, and gender roles are highly differentiated. Thus, the indications of these cultural dimension scores could guide a leader to adapt her style in leading a particular global organization.

## Organizational Learning

For many organizational research and leadership practices in the twenty-first century, one of the first questions asked to improve an existing system is how the organization can learn from both positive and negative situations. Even though the concept of organizational learning has different origins, identified essential foundations could specify basic definition for a uniform understanding. Argyris (1991) found that a more appropriate definition of organizational learning is to distinguish the consequences of organizational learning from the learning process. However, Senge (1990) argued that organizational learning entails leadership vision, communication, and teamwork within an organizational system. In an earlier study, Fiol and

Lyles (1985) conceptualized that organizational learning considers organizations as cognitive entities capable of observing their own actions, experimenting to discover the effects of alternative actions, and modifying actions to improve performance. With the various definitional perspectives, however, Senge's (1990) definition of organizational learning as a place of continual expansion of capacity in creating desired results, nurturing new and expansive patterns of thinking, and inspiring collective aspirations through continuous learning, is a working definition for this study.

Organizational learning is important in leadership because it is an interactive event that offers enthusiastic and humanistic solutions to complex problems plaguing organizations as they struggle in their effort in resolving those problems (Senge 1990, 1994). The enthusiastic and humanistic solutions have an ultimate goal of improving organizational situations (Knowles 1975; Senge 1994). The theoretical foundation underpinning leadership to organizational learning in this study is individual learning rates (Knowles 1975; Knox 1982) and single-loop/double-loop (Argyris 1976). According to Knox (1982), each individual in an organization learns at rates that are different from one another. Therefore, organizational learning should be tailored to meet individual learning needs and capabilities. Furthermore, organizational learning appears to explore both remote and immediate causes of organizational problems and devises means of resolving the problems by using new systems, designs, approaches, and methodologies (Dewey 1962; Senge 1994). Moreover, the law of association seems appropriate in organizational learning's exploratory process when leaders and followers work together as a team to unearth new facts, ideas, or concepts associated with known information (Knox 1982).

Argyris's (1976) single- and double-loop concepts explain how some factors are controlled in organizational decision making. *Single-loop learning* is correcting an action to solve or avoid a mistake. *Double-loop learning* is correcting underlying causes behind problematic action. Underlying causes include policies, assumptions, motives, informal practices, and so forth. They block inquiry on root causes in leadership decision making. Argyris (1976) found that organizational learning is instrumental in overcoming leadership implementation problems. Thus, leaders committed to organizational learning should find it essential to motivate followers to learn to achieve organizational efficiency and effectiveness. Organizational learning could also change potential behaviors (Levitt and March 1988). Since the learning process is channeled either formally and or informally, the process appears to enable organizations to acquire, access, and revise a system, as well as provide positive direction to organizational action and change (Miller 1993; Illeris 2003). Again, the leader with knowledge of organizational learning processes could distinguish organizational learning from other types of learning as well as interact among different levels of systems and analysis for effective results (Miller 1993).

Fundamentally, the leader could design structural arrangements throughout the learning process to guide positive change action (Miller 1993). Thus, the knowledge acquired through organizational learning could increase the organization's repertoire of positive change (Levitt and March 1988). Miller (1993) posited that organizational learning guides leaders to measure outcomes. Thus, a deviation in the process of measuring the outcome could be determined and corrective measures applied to remedy the situation for organizational efficiency and effectiveness. It is also important for organizational learning to link the present with the future in leadership (Robbins and Coulter 2012). According to Robbins and Coulter (2012), leaders should think of organizational learning as an extension of the past and an active invitation to future opportunities. Therefore, leaders should make organizational learning a way of life and actively support and encourage day-to-day improvements and changes for effective outcome.

Organizational learning concepts seem to provide avenues for exploring and understanding issues in organizations before major decisions are made (Senge 1990). Since organizational learning specifies types of events that constitute the learning process, its theoretical constructs could describe activities occurring over time for systematic leadership decision making (Crossan, Lane, and White 1999). Crossan et al.'s (1999) framework of organizational learning syncs with the author's personal philosophy:

(a) *Intuiting* (preconscious recognition of the possibilities inherent in the leader's personal experience)
(b) *Interpreting* (explanation of the idea to self and followers)
(c) *Integrating* (developing a shared understanding and coordinated action among fellow leaders and followers)
(d) *Institutionalizing* (ensuring that actions are made routine in the organization)

The expectation is that possible solutions to common organizational problems are intuitively processed with all possibilities on the table. Personal experience and wisdom acquired in leading organizations are major factors in the intuitive and interpreting processes. Peculiar understanding of the issue and expectations of how followers should understand the issues at stake are presented with a desire to seek followers' perspective.

The anticipation is to explore and seek common understanding with followers. It appears that when there is a common understanding among leaders and followers based on individual learning rates and hands-on common thoughtfulness, implementing change and institutionalizing new ideas could be a matter of time and space (Miettinen 2000). These organizational learning concepts are in line with Lewin's (1947) three-step change process of unfreeze, change, and refreeze. The leader with intuitive understanding could invariably persuade followers to agree that the status quo is not beneficial to them, thereby encouraging followers to view the problem from a new organizational learning perspective. Then, the leader and followers could work together on a quest for new, relevant information and connect views of the team together to support the change. The final phase is to focus on the new approach after lessons learned from the organizational learning process and integrate new institutionalized values through formal and informal mechanisms to stabilize the new equilibrium of change (Lewin 1947; Kritsonis 2005).

## Creating Effective Learning Organization.

Creating effective learning organization entails the use of a community of practice. Wegner, McDermott, and Snyder (2002) defined a community of practice as a group of people who share concerns, a set of problems or passions, and an intent to deepen knowledge and expertise through a regular learning interaction. Wegner et al. (2004) further argued that a community of practice catalyzes organizational democracy and engages followers to seek common solutions for problems they face. One measurable outcome of community of practice in organizational learning relates to increase in participants' professional capacity and control of organizational situations (Zuber-Skerritt 1992). For instance, a community of practice developed in an organization to solve marketing problems can work to implement and improve market offerings in products, services, experiences, and customer satisfaction. A good community of practice devised from organizational learning helps organizational marketers to set the right level of expectations for customers to meet customer value and customer satisfaction criterion in managing customer relationships (Kotler and Armstrong 2012). It is imperative for a leader to use Lewin's (1947) three-step change process as an organizational learning tool for positive outcome.

## Organizational Learning and Good Leadership Judgment

It appears that technical skills alone do not ensure effective organizational learning. The ability of the leader to apply good judgment also seems critical in today's organizational learning

(Raynolds and Ceranic 2007). According to Raynolds and Ceranic, good judgment is made up of experience, character, and curiosity. They further argued that experience allows leaders to see the rewards and consequences of their behavior, as well as that of others in the learning process. Character could serve as guidance, a moral compass to help leaders determine when something is important and within what personal boundaries to respond. Curiosity is also a part of human nature; leaders know that they never finish learning (Senge 1990). However, factors such as worldwide political changes, demographic changes, employee expectations, and increased globalization could fuel changes in organizations and leadership (Nahavandi 2009). Therefore, change is imminent in organizations and leadership. According to Morris, Brotheridge, and Urbanski (2005), good judgment in organizational learning is not something most leaders are born with; it is something they should continuously develop with extensive self-knowledge, morality, and humility.

Taylor (2004) emphasized that organizational learning is channeled through vision, communication, and teamwork to achieve desired change outcomes. This requires the leader to strike a fine balance in managing stakeholder interactions during the learning process. When leaders encourage followers in contributing and participating in the learning process, specific positive learning outcomes might well be addressed (Senge 1994).

The specific learning outcome is an interactive process derived from clarity, transparency, and specificity involved in the framing and pursuit of learning (Whitehead and McNiff 2006). Surprises should be expected in the learning process, because not all organizational learning outcomes are intended (Whitehead and McNiff 2006). However, with the right interactions, methods, content, intentions, and assessments, positive change could be effected and institutionalized in improving an organizational situation.

# Conclusion

As the world becomes more interdependent, complex, dynamic, and uncertain, comprehensive knowledge of all the domains analyzed in this chapter will guide a leader's understanding in working effectively in a globalized flat world. It is essential for organizational leaders to consider leadership in each domain's proper context and take into account the numerous factors that could affect the leader's personal authenticity, leadership process, and group or organizational performance. Globalization and multiculturalism seems to be the path of leaders' future because systems and global events influence leadership outcomes (Bird and Osland 2004; Daft 2009).

As believers in the deontological principles of Emmanuel Kant's law of categorical imperative, leaders must uphold right at all times and for all. In organizations, Kant's (1964) categorical principle should be a guideline against double standards in service and during the change process. For example, deception is considered unacceptable (Price 2006). Therefore, deception is equally an improper method of collecting information from followers, no matter how expedient the information might be.

Therefore, deceptive methods cannot be justified in any particular case of servant leadership, change, or governance situation, whether the leader is a private or public figure. The leader's goal is to ensure responsible use of the position entrusted into her care, uphold human dignity of followers, ensure fairness, and provide for a free flow information to all stakeholders.

Thus far, organizational leaders must have a supreme mission to serve. This service, far from implying servitude, instead means the willingness of leaders to be useful to followers, community, and country by being the first to serve others (Greenleaf 1992). In a globalized world, knowledge of the servant-as-leader mentality, ethics and governance, multiculturalism, organizational learning, change, innovation, and entrepreneurship must guide a leader to make a difference in a world of differences. It is in this light that these domains were chosen to enhance the leader's practice and influence.

# CHAPTER 3

## CONTACT YOURSELF

I do not forget that my voice is but one voice, my experience mere drop in the sea, my knowledge no greater than the visual field in a microscope, and my mind's eye a mirror that reflects a small corner of the world.

—C.G. Jung

Summers (2009) told a story of the president of an e-commerce firm who, after boasting of how wonderful his organization is, received an interesting proposal from a dissatisfied customer who had attended a meeting with the president: "If you think your company is so great, contact or call yourself." Feeling certain that the dissatisfied customer was exaggerating about the difficulties she might had experienced in contacting his organization, the president did just that. He placed a call to his own company. First, he visited the company's website. There, he selected the option labeled "Contact Us." When an e-mail box popped up on his computer screen, he typed in a question and sent it.

Three days later, he was still waiting for an answer.

He repeated the procedure. He sent another e-mail. He waited another three days.

Still there was no response for either e-mail. He finally located the customer service number and dialed the number during business hours. He received the following message: "You have reached customer service. Our regular business hours are 8:00 a.m. to 5:00 p.m. standard time. Please call back during regular business hours."

Since the manager was calling during regular business hours, the message surprised him. He tried pushing various buttons, including the zero button to speak to an operator. Much to his surprise, he was not able to contact his own company.

Are you surprised? That is how leadership is. If only leaders can call themselves.

One voice, a singular life experience, specialized knowledge, a clear vision, and a deeper thought are great tools in the world of leadership. Imagine after traveling abroad for over ten years, you finally return home, and your family asks, "How was your experience abroad for the past ten years?"

As simple as the question might be, a simplistic answer for a ten-year experience could be daunting, if not impossible. Leadership is similar to this long-years-travel experience. It is complex to memorize and decode complex life experiences that do not follow any pattern in a simple way for individuals who demand simple answers. Worse still, due to the concept of selective attention (which means our senses select events that we choose to pay attention to), unrehearsed experiences could be lost in short-term memories. Forgetfulness could also take place; more significantly, what is important to the traveler might not be important to the individual asking the seemingly simple but complex question.

Leadership hinges on the concept of complexity—of concepts, opinions, research methodologies, and theoretical frameworks. Many theories of leadership abound in organizations. However, in practice, leadership is situational (Northouse 2010). Different cultural context comes into play in the leader's ability to learn and understand employees, develop and manage relations, and manage overt and covert challenging situations. There seem to be many truths and possibilities in the personally acquired knowledge, intercultural competencies, and organizing expertise of leaders. However, it appears there are blind spots in leadership of which the leader could be ignorant. It is not the leader's fault; it is the nature of leadership. One open secret of leadership is ignorance. Ignorance of the leader in many dimensions of the organization he or she leads. Contemporary organizations place public responsibilities, citizenship, strategic planning and delegating, and consultative and directive responsibilities on the laps of organizational leaders. The leader is expected to be a workforce motivator who communicates effectively, provides feedback, tracks progress, and makes effective decisions. Further, the leader is expected to improve situations, commit to quality, create a customer focus, develop human resources and management, manage supplier relations, improve processes, use structured tools and techniques, manage projects, and achieve results.

However, leaders tend to know little about their own selves. They are sometimes ignorant of their own strengths and weaknesses. Ironically, some leaders also live in ignorance about their personal expectations and the feelings of their spouses and children. Is the concept of "knowing self and family" important in leadership? The answer is yes. Yet, many leaders lack the courage to admit that they need help. Why is this concept important in leadership? Leaders should begin to call themselves and hear the voice messages at the other end. An anonymous e-mail to ten close friends at various workplaces about what they think about this author and the subsequent response was enough to prove how most leaders don't know much about themselves, even though they pretend to know. It's a classic a mismatch of how some leaders see themselves and how employees see them. Why the mismatch?

There are many familiar and unfamiliar sounds that vibrate through leadership from homes and communities to the workplace. The home-community-workplace terrain is a familiar sight and sound leaders see and hear every day. The familiar sounds cuddle leaders between passion, people, places, technology, vision, and self-discipline. Constant association with personal passions, people, places, technology, vision, and behaviors could strengthen or weaken leadership. There are sounds of being ethical, creating a positive impression, trying to please followers and stakeholders, and yet, sounds of realizing that the more the leader learns from every situation, the more the leader realizes that she is ignorant about many issues at the workplace and even the immediate surroundings. That realization is not a negative thing. It is a compelling reason for realizing the need for change and for pursuing good leadership. The realization should spur the leader to appreciate that leadership is a journey of learning from every situation and circumstance. It is not a secret that in leadership, perceptions can be more important than reality. As stated earlier, followers could perceive different ideas from those of the leader. Until leaders can figure out the trend of change in these perceptions and change for the followers to perceive new positive thoughts (which syncs with the facts on the ground), followers may continue to see leaders in the light that has been created for them by the leaders.

# CHAPTER 4

## BE THE BEST IN TWO, AVERAGE IN TWO, AND COMPETITIVE IN TWO

Do not be daunted by the enormity of the world's grief. Do justly, now. Love mercy, now. Walk humbly, now. You are not obligated to complete the work, but neither are you free to abandon it.

—Talmud (Attributed)

Leadership literature has six pillars: knowledge, competency, disposition, skill, trait, and behavior. Research shows that being the best in two, average in two, and competitive in the remaining two are enough to be an effective leader in any organization. There are good reasons why people stay in their jobs. It may be that they like what they are doing and the people with whom they work. It may also be that they earn enough compensation to offset the stress and frustration of their job. Most employees have not come to terms with the reality that when they are happy, leadership is also happy because they (leaders) do not have to find someone to replace them. If we are happy at our jobs, our family is happy. Our clients are also happy because they do not miss our service. Our leaders are happy. Leaders are then positioned to make everyone—employees, clients, and all stakeholders—happy. That is the value employees are expected to bring to the table.

A leader's job is to demonstrate how different she is from the bunch of other leaders. She can do this by adding value through a created honest and trusting relationship. There are three major constructs that create honest and trusting work relationship between a leader and followers.

a) Do what you said you are going to do. For instance, if you said you will be at a meeting at 8:00 a.m., you have to be there at exactly the promised time. If for some reason you cannot be there, notify those likely to be affected by your absence in advance.

b) Communicate on a regular basis. Leaders should not only call followers when they need them to do something for them. Rather, call them on their birthdays to wish them well. Congratulate them even on achievements unrelated to work. The leader can send a simple e-mail or even a text message or move beyond regular conversations to ask followers of their family and plans they want to share. When leaders only call because they need something from followers, they (leaders) are not building honest and trusting relationship.

c) Exchange meaningful information. It is sensible for a leader to let subordinates know who she is. What are her interests, aspirations, weaknesses, and expectations? When a leader tells subordinates her weaknesses, they will know why she hired them, to complement her weaknesses. The sad thing that goes on in organizations and institutions is that most employees don't know how to handle shared leadership. The author observed a board meeting where the leader carefully assigned tasks to individuals she perceived to have expertise in those areas. During the meeting, she would often say, "We are trying to update our technology system here. Now, Sam, can you tell us your expectations for the new update?" It was clear to me that by the leader's actions, she was sharing responsibility, seeking new innovative ideas, and encouraging the heart of the employees to share their opinions, expectations, and fears. If followers share the same level of understanding with leaders in such situations, the outcome will be phenomenal.

The six pillars, again, come to the equation. To be on the generous side, leaders cannot be competitive in all six pillars: knowledge, competency, dispositions, skills, traits, and behaviors.

The proposal here is that the leader must specialize and compete. Experience and observations have shown that few leaders can successfully compete in all six pillars. The secret is to be the best in two, average in two, and competitive in the other two. For instance, if a leader has competitive advantage in knowledge and competency (note that knowledge of a job is different from being competent in a day-to-day operation), she could strive to be average in say, dispositions and skills, and competitive in traits and behaviors. The choice is not in any particular order, but the passion and interest of the leader is in gaining a competitive edge and staying ahead of the leadership game.

Leaders know their weaknesses—unless they don't want to admit to it. It can be lack of people skills or inadequate technical knowledge (all embedded in the six pillars). The truth is, most leaders exhibit just an average amount of core competency in leadership. Being competent in any of the two will enhance a leader's ability to capture, leverage and respond to situations to enhance talents and aptitudes at the workplace. While reflecting on these aptitudes, the leader should recognize that there are four major categories of people in every organization:

1. Those who enjoy talking about their peculiar problems
2. Those who seek more information about new ideas
3. Those who want to know how all new ideas fit in with their unique situation
4. Those who are willing to change by applying new ideas

Being on top of two of these categories, average in two, and competitive in the remaining two helps the leader to handle the four different types of individuals in organizations.

# CHAPTER 5

## EVERYBODY KNOWS A GOOD LEADER EXCEPT THE LEADER HERSELF

You cannot teach a man anything; you can only help him find it within himself.

—Galileo Galilee

Aristotle once said we are what we repeatedly do. When this "repeatedness" of behavior by either nature or nurture becomes a reinforced practice, learning takes place, and this guides individual behavioral and leadership styles. Nikki Giovanni stated that, "mistakes are a fact, and it is the response to error that counts." Leaders' errors (intended or otherwise) are easily picked by followers, who are always observing either from a distance or closely in everyday interactions. That is why there is the need for constant honest feedback to help leaders meet daily challenges. The author believes the normal "multirater feedback" is too formal in reviewing leaders' performance and proposes an informal approach where even customers, suppliers, or outsiders with interest in an organization could give leaders honest feedback. If walk-in individuals could fill out mini-survey forms about their first impression of the organization, it could go a long way in effecting change.

Experiences have shown that error is a source of transformation. That is why in the scientific world, most discoveries were unearthed by error. Teflon, for example, was discovered by accident in a process called *serendipity*. Besides minor unconscious errors leaders make at the workplace, it is also mostly difficult for one to know exactly what one is doing at any particular moment in time because forgetfulness is part of life. There is a proverb that says, "He who charts a path does not know his back is crooked unless someone tells him." This calls for feedback from informal sources, because the leader in most formal evaluations may be the final evaluator to give the assessment and evaluation the deserved weight or credibility. Thus the reason why many employees are careful to avoid undesired retaliation of some sort in evaluations. Common sense is applied here.

The leader has leverage in the employee's performance appraisal and career development, and a bad evaluation from the leader can seriously be an obstacle in the development of one's career. The next question is, what about all the collaborators who are evaluating the leader? The collaborators can be employees, contractors, customers, suppliers, governmental institutions, legal partners, and the communities (physical location) of our organization or institution. Since performance varies across contexts and cultures and individuals behave differently with different constituents, feedback from all collaborators and different constituents ensures reliability. The reason behind this is that the leader's performance is typically made up of multiple behaviors, and access to observing those different behaviors varies among constituencies. Multiple informal evaluations from different angles will capture this variance and improve leader's behavior and performance.

For more effective feedback, the leader can, as an alternative measure, invite entry-level workers, interns, or even students in institutions and begin an informal conversation of which aspects of the organization can be improved. The bottom line is to establish rapport by fitting into stakeholders' routines, finding common ground with them, and visiting them regularly in their cubicles, assembly lines, and lunchrooms. These are the areas where individuals speak of their frustrations, anger, and challenges—and make suggestions that will never appear in any suggestion box or 360-degree assessment. As an example, there was an organization the author consulted for that needed help in a change process of collaborating stakeholders in an international project. He begun by conducting a mini-survey with all the stakeholders to solicit desired "big ideas" and "big challenges" from each identified collaborator. On the way to his hotel room, the author picked up casual conversation with the official driver who told him he had been in that organization for eleven years, had watched everything unfolding, but also knew that his opinion in that organization had no substantial value. Apparently, the driver had witnessed all the four phases of the project and had driven many consultants to the same hotel many times. However, none of them bothered to ask his opinion about the organization he had been working for many years. Interestingly, most of the consulting recommendations came from that driver, rather than the "normal source," and the organization made great strides in the change process. The "hidden" challenge in that project was that previous consultants were "invisible" to the communities because they thought the communities had elected a board to represent them, and the consultants spent all their time with the board, not the communities.

According to the driver, the consultants' professional impression was that the board is the same as the community (because they were elected by the community to represent them in the project), but the community thought otherwise. The community wanted to meet the consultants personally to clarify technical issues and to resolve internal conflicts resulting from rumors going on in the community. Moreover, the internal consultants of the project had feelings of neglect because an external consultant (such as the author at that time) excluded them from the project's change process. In this case, objective feedback could not have been possible if the present consultant had not looked at the "unlikely source." Annon was right when he said, "If I keep an open mind, will my brain fall out?"

## SQRA Approach

The Specified Quick to Respond Approach (SQRA) is an innovative strategy for assisting willing and able employees to improve their services. The approach recognizes the existing capacity of employees to take responsibility for identifying and solving their everyday work problems. The approach holds potential for improvements in achieving employee satisfaction, sustainability, and source mobilization by reorienting employees to respond to organizational demands for improved services. The SQRA operates through a set of policies and project rules that are designed to create the incentives for employees to improve their input in a cost-effective and sustainable manner. It also empowers employees to initiate, choose, and implement a system that is able to elicit the appropriate response from sector actors and stakeholders.

Most leaders have a good idea of what works and what does not. In particular, policies of organizational economic and social good have to be managed at the lowest appropriate level to provide the foundation for the emergence of a new vision. The vision should be supported by an ongoing reorientation of broader policies involving commitment to stakeholders and reliance on their input to make the SQRA complete. Key characteristics of SQRA include the following:

(a) Employee capacity is appropriately strengthened and awareness raised by the quick response of both leaders and employees to issues.
(b) The approach should promote innovation and recognize the need for flexibility.
(c) Leaders and consultants should have a facilitative role, setting clear policies and strategies (including legal framework) that creates an enabling environment for all employees.
(d) The employees own and are responsible for sustaining projects and the physical facility. That is, treating every project or the company facility as if it is their own.
(e) Employees know how their level of service has significant impact on investment costs of the organization, both in relative and absolute terms.
(f) Employees initiate and make informed choices about service options and how extraordinary customer services are delivered.

## Challenges in Implementing SQRA
### Policy Implementation

It is necessary to strengthen policies and frameworks. Even where policies exist, there is often a lack of awareness and/or commitment to their implementation. These steps are recommended:

(a) Clarify or create clear policy and implementation mechanism—strategies, guidelines, legal framework, and regulations.
(b) Carry out awareness campaigns on policy/strategy, taking into consideration the time needed for acceptance of new ideas.
(c) Review the overall institutional set up and make necessary changes to support SQRA to enable all stakeholders to participate.
(d) Review procedures for procuring and channeling of funds in line with the needs of SQRA.

The adoption of SQRA should not be carried out in isolation but within the broader development context.

## Financing

One of the main constraints in implementing SQRA is the timely availability of funds. Other challenges include the following:

(a) Adopting financing mechanisms that create incentives for generation of funds
(b) Harmonizing financial-management methods between shareholders and stakeholders through adoption of coherent organizational development programs
(c) Providing a legal framework that encourages all actors to participate in financing and financial management of SQRA

(d) Developing mechanisms that enhance stakeholders' capabilities to manage, control, and direct financial resources in concert with the organizational vision

## Capacity Building

One of the challenges of implementing SQRA is the building of capacity at the different organizational levels, to respond to changes in approach. This is manifested in the lack of systems in most organizations to manage projects, inappropriate skills for system maintenance, inadequate skills to facilitate rather than implement employee initiatives, and the patronizing attitude of leaders toward employee development. In view of the magnitude of the challenges, there is the need for leaders to create an environment to accomplish the following:

(a) Strengthen the organization, improve leadership and organization skills, and upgrade technical skills in the organization
(b) Reorient leaders to manage and facilitate employee-initiated projects or ideas
(c) Focus on capacity at the lower level
(d) Sensitize leaders, consultants, politicians, and policymakers on SQRA

## The Way Forward

The way forward is to create a certain path of success through increased urgency and a demanding change. Below are some recommendations:

(a) Leaders should target interventions at both the employee and policy levels simultaneously. At the employee levels, carry out pilot projects that demonstrate the principle and its advantages. At the policy level, carry out awareness campaigns starting from upper management in order to involve shareholders and even policymakers in the promotion of SQRA.

(b) Develop project rules using your organizational experiences. This entails preparation and implementation of a learning agenda in current interventions and commitment to regular information exchange.

# CHAPTER 6

## THE BOUAZIZI FACTOR

There are numerous lessons leaders could learn from the uprising in the Arab world, from Algeria and Egypt in 2010 to the current uprising in Syria. One is found within the Bouazizi Factor.

Mohammed Bouazizi, twenty-six, was a poor and powerless man on the streets of Sidi Bouzid in Tunisia. He lived with his mother, stepfather, and six siblings in a modest studio in their home city of Sidi Bouzid, Central Tunisia. Bouazizi had more than once been arrested by the local police for doing business without a permit, even though the law does not require one for his kind of business.

His arrest and torture on December 7, 2010, at the hands of a Tunisian policewoman was destined to be his last. One hour after his arrest, Bouazizi set himself ablaze in front of a government building. He died eighteen days later at the Ben Arous Hospital, shortly after Tunisian then-president Ben Ali visited him. That marked the beginning of all the people's revolution in the Arab world. Ben Ali was ousted by the demonstration of the people after Bouazizi's death. He took shelter in Saudi Arabia. Egypt's Hosni Mubarak was the next to follow. Saudi Arabia, Sudan, Yemen, Mauritania, Iran, Jordan, Kuwait, Bahrain, Djibouti, Syria, and Libya are all had a feel of the Bouazizi Factor.

Colonel Moammar Gadhafi of Libya seized power through the barrel of a gun at twenty-seven. Forty-two years later, he met his untimely death in Libya when he tried to run away after the people revolted against him. Even the Saudi Arabian monarchy's grip of power had their roots shaken for the first time for reforms and people's representation. Bouazizi's short life story on this earth is indicative of deleterious leadership (both political and organizational) trends, where leaders enrich themselves at the backs of the poor or disrespect subordinates. Manual workers such as janitors, cleaners, and administrative assistants are mostly earning wages barely beyond the minimum wage. If this trend continues, organizations might experience similar incidents of Bouazizi's dramatic cry of revolution, where some workers could set themselves ablaze in front of offices to end the injustice in how individuals are paid in organizations. It seems to the author that change in wage structure for a living wage is a necessity for leadership. Organizations that respect all workers and show their respect with equitable pay structure, not for the executives alone, can flourish together. Employees do not want to be paupers in their own organization with a fifteen-cent-an-hour annual pay raise and meager bonuses, while top management shares all the profit and buys private jets and yachts. The principle of fairness applies here. Assume two individuals are given one hundred dollars to share; one takes ninety dollars and gives the other ten dollars. According to research, the fairness principle states that it is possible for the individual getting the ten dollars to reject the entire sum and go home with nothing because the division of the money is not fair. Logically, ten dollars are better than no dollars, yet the individual would rather get none than get an unfair share. Think about it!

# CHAPTER 7

# SYNCHRONICITY

One important thing most leaders experience in their everyday lives but do not attach any importance to is *synchronicity*. This is how synchronicity works: you think of a friend, and the next moment, she calls you, sends you an e-mail or a text message, or knocks at your door for a surprise visit. Human psychic and telepathic abilities are developing in ways that could be interesting if put into judicious use. We sometimes observe a conversation with an associate who brings forth an idea that you are planning to share and vice versa. This is the level of development expected when leaders do their homework well. Employees in the organization should gradually begin to communicate telepathically with one mission and one goal in the leader's shared vision. Thoughts should not be private, and telepathic communication should be the order of the day in our organizations.

Leaders need to remember that subordinates do not always operate on the same level of passion as leaders do. While leaders might feel (and it is true to a large extent) that they are responsible for anything that goes wrong in the organization, most subordinates may be quite relaxed on that "burden." That does not mean the subordinate's core competency is marginal. It only means leaders have not been able to bring their energy level to that of their employees. Synchronicity is lacking. This is how it works: When leaders open their minds to their followers to share a vision in a short and snappy way, even the simplest mind can understand. When they listen and share information about what needs to be done, leaders will be surprised. Perhaps as they rise from your office chair to pick a file, your personal assistant will rise simultaneously for the same purpose, as if the two had planned or discussed the issue already. When this level is attained, work becomes fun, and even private issues can be shared in a spirit of trust. Other benefits are numerous. First, turnover will reduce drastically, because what most leaders tend to forget is that some employees are not motivated by money alone. They seek relationship-building experiences. With synchronicity, it becomes very difficult for an employee to quit on a leader, even if there is a better offer somewhere.

If leaders can free their minds a little bit and stop being weighed down by assumptions of "being the boss," they can allow subordinates to do their best without always watching and monitoring what they say or do. They will be able to "churn out" better leaders than ourselves. That is because subordinates have the advantage of picking out the best leadership qualities to add to their own. The reason for this advice is clear: leaders are human. They may fall sick, attend to family responsibilities, or even go on vacation. Somebody will have to sit in the driver's seat in the leader's absence or be otherwise deputized. Most leaders have an inward fear that some subordinates might outshine them and take their position. This author even observed a situation that when a parking lot space allotted for a particular leader was used by a subordinate, the leader became infuriated. This thought process can create a toxic working environment for many great potential leaders. Most of these subordinates have no option but to quit the job, and the blame lies squarely on the leader's head. Leadership is over-glorified. The position must not get into a leader's head, because tomorrow, you might not hold the same position again.

Suffice it to say, every leadership idea comes from what the leader sees, hears, smells, touches, tastes, or even senses. Such ideas can be conceived, but to become useful and valid, the ideas need to be placed in relevant context that has been tested by what individual group members think about that idea. The logical comparison that follows is in what happens when two people dance. They spin, twirl, flip, somersault, and they do it more or less together. Do they hear the same music? The answer could be yes, but they don't hear the same beat of the same music. That is why the dancing moves differ.

This chapter ends with an important concept of another academic and practical difference between leaders and managers that needs to be addressed. The table below highlights some of the role differences.

*Table 1:*

Differences between Leaders and Managers

| Leader | Manager |
|---|---|
| Goal oriented | Task oriented |
| Position achieved | Position given |
| Horizontal | Vertical |
| Takes risk | Manages risk |
| Earns respect | Demands respect |
| Collaborates | Leads |
| Open minded | Closed minded |
| Innovative | Antiquated |
| Visionary | Structured |
| Intuitive | Logical |
| Inspires | Instructs |
| Empowers | Controls |
| Pursues dreams | Performs duties |
| Wonders why | Asks how |
| Develops people | Develops products |

At a cursory look, the table above makes sense, because every leadership student has gone through the rudiments of these seeming differences. However, recent studies have found limitations in the differences. Testing forms of leadership literature and behaviors from multiple theoretical studies (Hannah, Sumanth, Lester, and Cavarretta 2014) revealed different theoretical thoughts. As an example, Hannah et al. (2014) argued that: "The promulgated false separation between leadership and management is thus not ecologically valid and can promote perceptions in the casual observer that leadership is just about the 'soft stuff' and making followers feel good. Instead, leadership should be viewed as being functional and a multiplier of managerial functions and effectiveness" (p. 603).

Hannah et al. further gave an example of a classical management function such as planning, where a manager can lay out her goals and objectives in ways that are more or less inspiring, charismatic, or visionary, which also emphasizes ethical implications of the planned activity (p. 603). From the given example, management and leadership are blended in achieving a common goal for an organization. Another example is the management function of organizing. Evidently, a manager can organize work activities by considering levels of individual employee talents, needs, and desires to such an extent that the organizing process leads to the promotion of talents and co-leaders and who can achieve similar results in the manager's absence. Have we not blended the two, management and leadership, in the process?

Thus, leadership reflects ways in which management is enacted, and it is a false dichotomy to separate the two (Hannah et al. 2014). Leadership and management, therefore, could be synchronized in academia and practice.

# CHAPTER 8

# BE THE JUDGE

Be the judge in the three scenarios below. Organizations and students in group work could role-play or conduct open discussions of these scenarios.

## Scenario 1: What Do You Want Me to Do?

Alice (not her real name) remembers fuming over a caution letter she received as a management consultant from her team leader in an international project. The issue was that her official driver forgot to lock the company's car doors over the weekend. This particular vehicle was parked at the office on Friday evening when Alice was on a field trip with another driver, and the team leader noticed the unlocked car doors the following Monday morning before Alice reported to work. This was Alice's reply to the project team leader's caution letter:

> I think your letter is misdirected, misconstrued, and quite unfair to me. As you are aware, on the day in question when the car was unlocked, I was on a field trip with another official car due to a mechanical fault on mine. The official driver of the "unlocked car" had earlier detected a mechanical fault and sent the vehicle to a mechanic. After the mechanic had fixed the problem, he parked the car in front of the office on Friday evening and kept the keys because the office

was closed at the time the mechanic finished fixing the car. I was not in town or at the office at that time. This driver did not report to me of any further problems on the repaired car, either on phone or e-mail over the weekend. This morning, in response to your caution letter, I in turn gave the driver a caution letter to explain what happened and in his reply (attached), he stated that after servicing the vehicle on Friday evening, he only realized when leaving the office that the central lock of the car was not working. I was not in the know of such a situation until I received your caution letter this morning. When I further questioned the driver, he apologized attributing it to forgetfulness and family issues that were bothering him last Friday. I believe the driver was hired on his professional merit and should be accountable for explaining his actions before the issue comes to me. In this case, it should have been established whether I knew of the incident before I was cautioned. As it stands now, the impression being created is as if I am responsible for the unlocked vehicle. I would have wished we resolve this problem verbally, not with a caution letter.

After two days, Alice received this response from her project team leader:

We have received your response to the caution letter. In the case of the unlocked vehicle, you did not ensure that the driver lived to his responsibilities. You are to ensure that this lapse do not occur again in the future. Your explanation is unacceptable. You are reminded that the project's regulations on use of vehicles will be applied and further sanctions would be taken should this action be repeated.

## Scenario 2: My Boss Let Me Down

John Smith has been an employee in a particular grocery store for fifteen years, working as a cashier. He also picked up any additional jobs assigned to him. Recently, John had a disagreement with a customer in a sales transaction. After a couple of days, John's manager told him that her investigation into the issue had a result that "seemed" to be John's fault. Based on the organization's employment policy with customers, John was fired. A polygraph test was an offer of a second chance to prove his innocence. This was necessary because of the word "seemed" used in the investigatory process. John was not coerced to take the polygraph test. He did it to defend his integrity and the hard-won reputation he had earned after fifteen years at the grocery store. Even though the polygraph result was positive, polygraphs are not generally considered reliable. John insisted on his innocence, but his boss faulted him and held John responsible and accountable for his uncontrolled action, in accordance with the organization's policies, before being fired. John sued both his boss and the organization for unfair treatment, but the court ruled that he was legally, procedurally, and rightfully terminated, stating that John willfully agreed to take the polygraph test without being coerced. John always felt his boss let him down.

**Scenario 3: This Is How I Feel**

Beth had been an administrator at a local insurance company for eighteen years. She lost her job recently due to downsizing but was able to find a new job with another financial institution.

After she had been trained on the job, Beth felt she was starting a great career, until she realized that her immediate supervisor, either consciously or unconsciously, was too assertive and micromanaged every activity at the workplace. Beth sensed a manipulative attitude from her boss. She felt that unless some of the procedures are policy requirements, most of the regular daily routines should be done based on the employee's own value judgment or discretion. For instance, the boss would tell Beth to do photocopying one way, when Beth thought she could do it another way and get the same results. After a couple of weeks, Beth gathered the courage to tell her boss that she felt inferior when the boss tried to instruct her on even the most routine processes of the organization. The boss took offense at Beth's comment and developed a cold attitude toward her. Beth felt sorry for not harboring her feelings, and she resigned after nine months.

# CHAPTER 9

# THE LEGAL SIN

Most leaders do not like sexual-harassment training (including the author). However, this legal sin can end every leader's career and crumble years of hard-won reputation. Sexual harassment, sex scandals, and extramarital affairs have brought many great men and women leaders to their knees, while negating the reputation they have used all the energy of their lifetimes to build. If you struggle with the legal sin, you're not alone.

Former Detroit mayor Kwame Kilpatrick, on the other hand, denied everything from the beginning. The list is endless, and it is one on which you don't want to be listed. Image is everything in leadership. But for privacy, most human resources will tell thousands of sexual-harassment stories at the rooftop. Thousands of similar stories are either not reported or swept under the rug. But with time, they will come up, sometimes five or even ten years after the fact. A former neighbor, a project manager at a Fortune 100 company in the United States for thirteen years, was recently fired from his job for sexual harassment. Worse still, his church also excommunicated him within a six-month period for sleeping with multiple married women in the church. Sex, they say, is legal. However, it is only in legal sin that ethics supersedes legality in all the cases mentioned in this chapter. Can you imagine the effect of a sex scandal involving you— yes, you? That is the extent to which a few minutes of uncontrolled pleasure-seeking behavior can unmake great leaders. For the avoidance of doubt, Google or search YouTube for sexual scandals, and be the judge of the weight of disgrace on the individuals involved. The next spotlight may be on you!

# REFERENCES

Adler, N. J. *International Dimensions of Organizational Behavior* (Second Edition). Belmont: Wadsworth, 1991.

Adler, N. J. *Global Leadership: Women Leaders*. In M. Mendenhall, T. Kuhlmann, and G. Stahl (eds.). *Developing Global Business Leaders, Policies, Processes, and Innovations*. Westport, CT: Quorum Books, 2001).

Adler, N. J., and S. Bartholomew. "Managing Globally Competent People." *Academy of Management Executive*, 6, (1992): 52–65.

Anderson, P. (1999). Complexity Theory and Organizational Science. *Organizational Science, 10* (1), 6-23.

Antal, A. B., Dierkes, M., Child, J., and Nonaka, I. (2001). Organizational Learning and Knowledge: Reflections on the Dynamics of the Field and Challenges for the Future. In Dierkes, M., Antal, A.B., Child, J. and Nonaka, I. (Eds.), *Handbook of Organizational Learning and Knowledge* (pp. 921-39). New York: Oxford University Press.

Argyris, C. and D. A. Schon. *Organizational Learning*. Reading, MA: Addison-Wesley, 1978.

Argyris, C. (May-June 1991). Teaching Smart People How to Learn. *Harvard Business Review*, 99-109.

Badaracco, J. L. (2002). *Leading Quietly: An Unorthodox Guide to Doing the Right Thing*. Harvard Business Review Press, Boston, MA.

Bailey, J., and Axerold, R. H. (2001). Leadership Lessons from Mount Rushmore: An Interview with James MacGregor Burns. *Leadership Quarterly, 12*(1), 113-127.

Bass, B. M., and Avolio, B. J. (1994). *Improving Organizational Effectiveness Through Transformational Leadership*. Thousand Oaks, CA: Sage.

Bass, B. M., and Bass, R. (2008). *The Bass Handbook of Leadership: Theory, Research, and Managerial Applications* (4th ed.). New York, NY: Free Press.

Bellman, G. M. (2002). *The Consultant's Calling: Bringing Who You Are to What You Do*. San Francisco, CA: Jossey-Bass.

Black, S. J., and Gregerson, H. B. (2015). *It Starts with One: Changing Individuals Changes Organizations* (3rd ed.). Upper Saddle River, NJ: Pearson Education.

Bird, A. (October 2011). *Global Leadership*. Seminar for doctoral students in organizational leadership. Indiana Wesleyan University, IN: Marion.

Bird, A., and Osland, J. (2004). Global Competencies: An Introduction. In H. Lane, M. Maznevski, M. Mendenhall and J. McNett (eds.). *Handbook of Global Management*. Oxford: Blackwell: 57-80.

Boa, K. (2001). *Confined to His Image*. Grand Rapids, MI: Zondervan.

Brown, J. S., and Duguid, P. (1991). Organizational Learning and Communities-of-Practice: Toward a Unified View of Working, Learning, and Innovation. *Organizational Science, 2*, 40-57.

Brown, M. E., and Trevino, L. K (2006). Ethical Leadership: A Review and Future Directions. *The Leadership Quarterly, 17*(1), 595-616. doi: 10.1016/j.leaqua.2006.10.004

Bryman, A. 2006. Paradigm Peace and the Implications for Quality. *International Journal of Social Research Methodology 9*, 111–126.

Burnes, B. (2004). Kurt Lewin and the Planned Approach to Change: a Reappraisal. *Journal of Management Studies 46*(6), 1-26.

Burns, J. M. (1978). *Leadership*. New York: Harper and Row.

Caldwell, R. (2005). Things Fall Apart? Discourse on Agency and Change in Organizations. *Human Relations, 58*(1), 83-114.

Cameron, K. S., and Quinn, R. E. (2006). Diagnosing and Changing Organizational Culture: Based on the Competing Values Framework (Rev. ed.). San Francisco, CA: Jossey-Bass.

Carter, C., Bishop, J., and Kravits, S. L. (2012). *Keys to Success: Building Analytical, Creative, and Practical skills* (7th ed.). Boston, MA: Allyn and Bacon.

Chaleff, I (March 2012). *The Courageous Follower: Standing Up to and for Our Leaders*. Seminar for Masters in Organizational Leadership, College of Mount St. Joseph, Cincinnati, OH.

Chan, A. (2005). Authentic Leadership Measurement and Development: Challenges and Suggestions. In W. L. Gardner, B. J. Avolio, and F. O. Walumbwa (Eds.). *Authentic Leadership Theory and Practice: Origins, Effects, and Developments* (pp. 227-251). Oxford: Elsevier Science.

Cohen, R. W. (2009). *Snapshots of God*. Review and Herald Publishing Association.

Coombs, W. T. (2004). Impact of Crises in Organizational Communications: Insights from Situational Crisis Communication Theory. *Journal of Business Communication*, 41(*1*), 265-289.

Covey, S. (2015). *The 7 Habits of Highly Effective People*. Mango Media Inc.

Crossan, M., Lane, H. W., and White, R. E. (1999). An Organizational Learning Framework: From Intuition to Institution. *Academy of Management Review, 24*(3), 522-537.

Cuilla, J. (March 2012). *Current Trends in Leadership: Philosophy and Leadership*. Seminar for doctoral students in organizational leadership. Indiana Wesleyan University, Indianapolis, IN

Cuilla, J. B. (2001). Carving Leaders from the Warped Wood of Humanity. *Canadian Journal of Administrative Sciences, 18*(4), 313-319.

Cuilla, J. B. (2005). The State of Leadership Ethics and the Work that Lies before Os. *Business Ethics: A European Review, 14*(4), 323-335.

Daft, R. L. (2008). *Organizational Theory and Design* (10th ed.). Mason, OH: South-Western.

Daft, R. L. (2009). *Organizational Theory and Design* (11th ed.). Mason, OH: South-Western.

Day, D. V. (2000). Leadership Development: A Review in Context. *Leadership Quarterly, 11* (1), 581-613.

Dewey, J. (1962). *A Centennial Bibliography*. Chicago: University of Chicago Press.

Dimitriadis, G., and McCarthy, C. (2000). Globalizing Pedagogies: Power, Resentment, and the Re-narration of Differences. In Ram Mahalingam and Cameron McCarthy (eds). *Multicultural Curriculum: New Directions for Social Theory, Practice, and Policy*. New York: Routledge.

Drucker, P. F. (1996). *The Leader of the Future*. San Francisco: CA: Jossey-Bass.

Dumbar, R. L. M., and Starbuck, W. H. (2006). Learning and Designing Organizations and Learning from Designing Them. *Organizational Science, 17*(2), 171-178.

Dunoon, D. (2008). *In the Leadership Mode: Concepts, Practices, and Tools for a Different Leadership*. London: Trafford Publishing.

Early, P. C., and Ang, S. (2003). *Cultural Intelligence: Individual Interactions across Cultures*. Palo Alto, CA: Stanford University Press.

Easterby-Smith, M., Crossan, M., and Nicolini, D. (2000). Organizational Learning: Debates Past, Present, and Future. *Journal of Management Studies 37*(1), 96-783.

Evans, M. G. (1996). R. J. House's "A Path-Goal Theory of Leader Effectiveness." *Leadership Quarterly, 7*(3), 305-309.

Fielding, J. L., and Gilbert, N. (2006). *Understanding Social and Organizational Statistics* (2nd ed.). London: Sage.

Fiol, M. C., and Lyles, M. A. (1985). Organizational Learning. *Academy of Management Review, 10*(4), 803-813.

Galford, R., and Drapeau, A. S. (2003). The Enemies of Trust. *Harvard Business Review, 81*(2), 89-93.

George, B. (2003). *Authentic Leadership: Rediscovering the Secrets to Creating Lasting Values*. San Francisco: Jossey-Bass.

Goldstein, J. (2006). Emergence, Creative Process, and Self-Transcending Constructions. In K. Richardson (ed.),

*Managing Organizational Complexity: Philosophy, Theory, and Applications.* ISBN 978-1593113193, pp. 63-78.

Goleman, P. G. (1997). *Emotional Intelligence.* New York: Batman Books.

Greenleaf, R. K. (1977). *The Servant as a Leader.* New Jersey: Paulist Press.

Greenleaf, R. K. (1991). *The Servant Leader.* Westfield, IN: The Robert Greenleaf Center

Greenleaf, R. K. (1998). *The Power of Servant Leadership.* San Francisco, CA: Berrett-Koehler.

Gunderman, R. (September 2011). *Leadership: Command, Contract, or Covenant? Seminar for Doctoral Students in Organizational Leadership.* Indiana Wesleyan University, Indianapolis, IN.

Hannah, S. T., Sumanth, J. J., Lester, P., and Cavarretta, F. (2014). Debunking the False Dichotomy of Leadership and Pragmatism: Critical Evaluation and Support of Newer Genre Leadership Theories. *Journal of Organizational Behavior, 35*(1), 598-621. doi: 10.1002/job.1931

Hall, E. T. (1973). *The Silent Language.* Garden City, NY: Anchor Press, Doubleday.

Harrison, R. (2010). Bringing Your Spiritual Practice into Your Work. *ReVision, 30*(3/4), 107-117. doi: 10.4298/REVN.30.3.4.107-117

Harshman, C. L., and Harshman, E. F. (2008). The Gordian Knot of Ethics: Understanding Leadership Effectiveness and Ethical Behavior. *Journal of Business Ethics, 78*(1), 175-192. doi: 10.1007/s10551-006-9318-8

Hazy, J. K., and Silberstang, J. (2009). Leadership within Emergent Events in Complex Systems: Micro-enactments and the Mechanisms of Organizational Learning and Change. *The International Journal of Learning and Change, 3*(3), 230-247.

Hofstede, G. (2001). *Culture's Consequences: Comparing Values, Behaviors, Institutions, and Organizations across Organizations.* Beverly Hills, CA: Sage.

Hogg, M. A. (2001). The Social Identity Theory of Leadership. *Personality and Social Psychology Review, 5*(1), 184-200.

Hurst, D. (1995). *Crisis and Renewal: Meeting the Challenges of Organizational Change*. Boston, Mass.: Harvard Business School Press.

Hussey, T., and Smith, P. (2003). The Uses of Learning Outcomes. *Teaching in Higher Education, 8*(3), 357-368. doi: 10.1080/1356251032000088574

Illeris, K. (2003). Towards a Contemporary and Comprehensive Theory of Learning. *International Journal of Lifelong Education, 22*(4), 396-406.

James, E. A. (2005). Prospects for the Future: Use of Participatory Action Research to Study Issues of Educational Disadvantage. *Journal of Irish Educational Research, 24*(2-3) 199-206.

James, E. A., Milenkiewicz, M. T., and Bucknam, A. (2008). *Participatory Action Research for Educational Leadership: Using Data-Driven Decision Making to Improve Schools*. Thousand Oaks, CA: Sage.

Johnson, C. E. (2007). *Ethics in the Workplace: Tools and Tactics for Organizational Transformation*. Thousand Oaks, CA: Sage Publications Inc.

Kant, E. (1964). *Groundwork of the Metaphysics of Morals* (ed.). New York: Harper and Row Publishers.

Kellerman, B. (2004). *Bad Leadership: How It Is, How It Happens, Why It Matters*. Boston, MA: Harvard Business School Press.

Kevany, K. D. (2008). Building the Requisite Capacity for Stewardship and Sustainable Intertemporal Stewardship Theory. *Managerial Finance, 33*(12), 970-979. doi:10.1108/03074350710831747

Klann, G. (2007). *Building Character: Strengthening the Heart of Good Leadership*. San Francisco, CA: Jossey-Bass.

Knowles, M. S. (1975). *Self-Directed Learning: A Guide for Learners and Teachers*. Englewood Cliffs: Cambridge.

Knox, A. B. (1982). Organizational Dynamics in University Continuing Professional Education. *Adult Education Quarterly, 32*(3), 117-129. doi: 10.1177/074171368203200301

Kotler, P., and Armstrong, G. (2012). *Principles of Marketing*. Upper Saddle River, NJ: Pearson Prentice Hall.

Kotter, J. P. (2002). *Leading Change*. Boston: Harvard Business School Press.

Kotter, J. P., and Cohen, D. S. (2002). *The Heart of Change: Real Life Stories of How People Change Their Organizations*. Boston, MA: Harvard Business Press.

Kouzes, J. M., and Posner, B. Z. (1993). *Credibility: How leaders Gain and Lose It, Why People Demand It*. San Francisco, CA: Jossey-Bass.

Kozai Group (2009). *The Global Competency Inventory*. St. Louis, MO: Kozai.

Kozlowski, S., Chao, G., and Jensen, J. (2010). Building an Infrastructure for Organizational Learning: A Multilevel Approach. In S. Kozlowski, and E. Salas, *Learning, Training, and Development in Organizations* (pp. 363-404). New York: Routledge.

Kritsonis, A. (2005). Comparison of Change Theories. *International Journal of Scholarly Academic Intellectual Diversity, 8*(1), 1-7.

Lambert, L. (2009). *Spirituality Inc.*: Religion in the American Workplace. New York, NY: New York University Press.

Latour, B. (2000). When Things Strike Back: A Possible Contribution of Science Studies to the Social Sciences. *British Journal of Sociology, 51*(1), 107-123.

Levitt, B., and March, J. G. (1988). Organizational Learning. *Annual Review of Psychology*, 319-340.

Lewin, K. (1947). Frontiers in Group Dynamics. *Human Relations, 1*(1), 5-41.

Longenecker, J. G., Petty. W. J., and Palich, L. E., and Hoy, F. (2012). *Small Business Management: Launching and Growing Entrepreneurial Ventures*. Mason, OH: South-Western

Mendhall, M. E., Osland, A. L. Bird, A., Oddou, G. R., and Maznevski, M. L. (2008). *Global Leadership: Practice and Development*. New York, NY: Routledge.

Miettinen, R. (2000). The Concept of Experiential Learning and John Dewey's Theory of Reflective Thought Action.

*International Journal of Lifelong Education* 19(1), 54-72. doi: 10.1080/026013700293458.

Miller, D. (1993). The Architecture of Simplicity. *Academy of Management Review, 18*(1), 116-138.

Mintzberg, H. (2004). Leadership and Management Development. An Afterword. *Academy of Management Executive*, 18(3), 140-142.

Morris, J. A., Brotheridge, C. M., and Urbanski, J. C. (2005). Bringing Humility to Leadership: Antecedents and Consequences of Leader Humility. *Human Relations, 58*, 1323-1350.

Mumford, M. D. (2006). *Pathways to Understanding Leadership: A Comparative Analysis of Charismatic, Ideological, and Pragmatic Leaders.* Mahwan, NJ: Lawrence Erlbaum.

Nahavandi, A. (2009). *The Art and Science of Leadership* (5th ed.). Upper Saddle River, NJ: Pearson Prentice Hall.

Northouse, P. (2010). *Leadership: Theory and Practice* (5th ed.). Thousand Oaks, CA: Sage Publications.

Northouse, P. G. (2010). *Leadership: Theory and Practice* (6th ed.). Thousand Oaks, CA: Sage.

Novak, M. (1996). *Business as a Calling.* New York, NY: The Free Press.

Papert, S. (2000). What's the Big Idea? Toward a Pedagogy of Power. *IBM Systems Journal* 39(3/4), 720—729.

Pirie, W. L., and McCuddy, M. K. (2007). A Preliminary Test of the Validity of a Proposed

Powell, C. (1995). *My American Journey.* New York: Random House.

Price, T. L. (2006). *Understanding Ethical Failures in Leadership.* Cambridge, NY: Cambridge University Press.

Reynolds, S. J., and Ceranic, T. L. (2007). The Effects of Moral Judgment and Moral Identity on Moral Behavior: An Empirical Examination of the Moral Individual. *Journal of Applied Psychology, 92*, 1610-1624.

Robbins, S. P., and Coulter, M. (2012). *Management* (11th ed.). Upper Saddle River, NJ: Pearson Education, Inc.

Robert, T. K. (2012). *Rich Dad, Poor Dad.* Scottsdale, AZ: Plata Publishing.

Rowold, J., and Heinitz, K. (2007). Transformational and Charismatic Leadership: Assessing the Convergent, Divergent, and Criterion Validity of the MLQ and the CKS. *Leadership Quarterly, 18*(1), 121-133

Sargut, G., and McGrath, R. G. (2011). Learning to Live with Complexity. *Harvard Business Review, 89*(9/10), 68-76.

Schein, E. H. (2010). *Organizational Culture and Leadership* (4th ed.). San Francisco, CA: Jossey-Bass.

Schein, E., H. (2004). *Organizational Culture and Leadership*. Wiley Publications.

Schumann, P. L. (2001). A Moral Principles Framework for Human Resources Management Ethics. *Human Resources Management Review, 11*(1/2), 93-111.

Schwartz, M. S., (2003). Corporate Social Responsibility: A Three-Domain Approach. *Business Ethics Quarterly, 13*(4), 503-530.

Senge, P. (1999). Learning for a Change. *Fast Company, 24*(1), 85-178.

Senge, P. M. (1990). *The Fifth Discipline: The Art and Practice of the Learning Organization*. New York, NY: Doubleday.

Senge, P. M. (1994). *The Fifth Disciple Fieldbook: Strategies and Tools for Building a Learning Organization*. New York: Doubleday.

Solansky, S. T. (2008). Leadership Style and Team Processes in Self-Managed Teams. *Journal of Leadership and Organizational Studies, 14*(4), 332-341.

Spears, L. C. (1995). *Reflections and Leadership*. New York: John Wiley and Sons.

Spears, L. C. (2002). Character and Servant Leadership: Ten Characteristics of Effective and Caring Leaders. *Journal of Virtues and Leadership, 1*(1), 25-30.

Stacey, R. D. (2001). *Complex Responsive Processes in Organizations: Learning and Knowledge Creation*. London: Routledge.

Stewart, I., and Joines, V. (1991). *TA Today: A New Introduction to Transactional Analysis*. Chapel Hill, NC: Lifespace.

Summers, D. C. S. (2009). *Quality Management: Creating and Sustaining Organizational Effectiveness* (2nd ed.). Upper Saddle River, Columbus, OH.

Tannenbaum, R., and Schmidt, W. (1986). HBR Highlights: Excerpts of How to Choose a Leadership Pattern. *Harvard Business Review*, 131.

Taylor, S. E. (2004). Escape from Reality: Illusions in Everyday Life. In B. M. Staw (Ed.), *Psychological Dimensions of Organizational Behavior* (3rd ed.). New York: Pearson.

Ticky, N., Brimm, M., Charan, R., and Takeuchi, H (1992). Leadership Development as a Lever for Global Transformation. In V. Pucik, N. Tichy, and C. K. Barnett (eds.). *Globalization Management: Creating and Leading the Competitive Organization*. New York: John Wiley.

Tosi, H. L. (2009). *Theories of Organization*. Thousand Oaks, CA: Sage Publications.

Trevino, L. K., Brown, M. E., and Hartman, L. P. (2003). A Qualitative Investigation of Perceived Executive Ethical Leadership: Perceptions from Inside and Outside the Executive Suite. *Human Relations, 55*(1), 5-37.

Valk, J. (2009). Knowing Self and Others: Worldview Study. *Journal of Adult Theological     Education, 6*(*1*), 69-80. doi: 10.1558/jate2009v6i1.69

Van Vugt, M. (October 13 2011). *Presentation at the Thirtieth Annual Meeting of the Association for Politics and the Life Sciences*, Cincinnati, OH: Garfield Suites Hotel

Van Vugt, M., and Ahuja, A. (2011). *Naturally Selected: The Evolutionary Science of Leadership*. New York: Harper Collins.

Weber, M. (1946). *From Max Weber: Essays in Sociology* (ed.), Hans H. Gerth and C. Wright Mills. New York: Oxford University Press.

Weber, M. (1947). *The Theory of Social and Economic Organization* (ed.), A. Henderson and T. Parsons. Glencoe, IL: Free Press.

Wegner, E., McDermott, R. A., and Snyder, W. (2002). *Cultivating Communities of Practice: A Guide to Managing Knowledge*. Boston: Harvard Business School Press.

Whitehead, J., and McNiff, J. (2006). *Action Research: Living Theory*. London: Sage.

Yip, G.S. (1995). *Tot and Global Strategy: Managing for Worldwide Competitive Advantage.* (Business school edn.). Englewood Cliffs, NJ: Prentice Hall.

Zaccaro, S. J. (2007). Trait-Based Perspectives of Leadership. *American Psychologist, 62*(1), 6—16.

Zuber-Skerritt, O. (1992). *Professional Development in Higher Education: A Theoretical Framework of Action Research.* London: Kogan Page.